BEGINNER'S GUIDE TO RIDING

Veronica Heath

Veronica Heath's practical approach clarifies
and helps overcome the problems facing the
novice rider when she encounters her first
pony. She provides an invaluable guide for
those taking lessons and for those about to
own a pony, giving common-sense advice on
choosing, feeding, stabling, riding and
generally deriving the greatest enjoyment
from riding. Special attention is paid to the
modern problems of riding in built-up areas
and traffic, and to the growth of Pony and
Riding clubs offering even greater possibilities
for those who enjoy being in the saddle.

This book is an indispensable guide to help
every novice rider achieve competence and
skill.

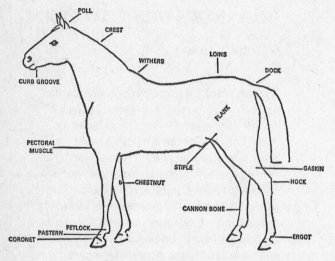

Fig. 1. Points of the horse

BEGINNER'S GUIDE TO RIDING

Beginner's Guide to Riding

VERONICA HEATH

SPHERE BOOKS LIMITED
30/32 Gray's Inn Road, London, WC1X 8JL

First published in Great Britain in 1971 by Pelham Books Ltd.
© Veronica Heath, 1971
First Sphere Books edition 1973

TRADE
MARK

Set in Intertype Baskerville

Printed in Great Britain by
Hazell Watson & Viney Ltd,
Aylesbury, Bucks

CONTENTS

CHAPTER ONE

RIDING – WHAT THE SPORT CAN OFFER A YOUNG PERSON TODAY

Riding has now become a national pastime and horses have become a recreation to an increasing number of people. It is no longer only the rich who can afford to ride. Men, women and children from almost every walk of life are now able to indulge in this delightful form of sport. Facilities are available in towns as well as country, for beginners, and for the experienced, and more and more people are taking advantage of this.

Through the medium of television, which brings racing and show jumping into every home, interest is stimulated further and it is easy for enthusiasts to study the experts. Good riding establishments and, unfortunately, some bad ones too, report record bookings. People are discovering that it is one of the most enjoyable ways of taking exercise.

For the majority, however, riding does not come by nature. It is true that there are a few natural horsemen about, but even these fortunates had to learn at the beginning. When to begin and, where to begin, and what it is all going to cost, are important considerations for the amateur. Riding schools, riding clubs and equestrian centres are numerous, and what they have to offer the novice is valuable only if the right course is chosen which will adequately fit the recipient, physically and financially. Naturally, the ideal is to own a horse yourself. Particularly, this is true for children because most young people love animals and the country, and unless this love is fostered it may be lost as they grow older.

But there are pitfalls as well as pleasures in store for the horse owner, however, and these must be avoided as far as possible.

Before the decision is taken to learn to ride, it is necessary to consider what the sport will have in store for you in the future. If you live in the country and the neighbouring farmers are congenial and you have friends who ride, your prospects are excellent. There is a good chance that you should be able to ride fairly inexpensively and with the maximum of enjoyment. If you can afford it, you will also be able to enjoy hunting which is the most wonderful way to see the countryside, meet friends with the same interests as yourself and indulge in some very healthy exercise.

But if you live in a built-up area, in the centre of a town or on a busy main road, the question of whether to learn to ride will be a more serious one. Because your riding will be much more expensive and may, possibly, be restricted to organised riding at a school, or centre, because the pleasures of ownership may be too complicated and expensive to make the acquisition of your own animal worthwhile. Exercising a horse along a busy thoroughfare today is not only a tiresome chore, it can also be highly dangerous. Where it used to be merely rather boring trotting down the roads where no nice fields and lanes welcomed riders, it has now become a salutary experience for the horse owner. This is the age of speed and there is scant provision for any form of equestrianism on our modest highways. Too many young children today have had their nerve shattered by a fall on tarmac. The quietest pony can shy and no parent should allow a young child alone on a pony on a busy road.

Nevertheless, there is hope for the town-dweller. More now, I think, than there has ever been. Riding clubs have been formed – there are two hundred of them all over the country – and really good riding schools and centres have now been opened.

Let us consider what is the right age to begin to ride. Not, necessarily, at the tender age of three years, trailing about on a donkey. Too many enthusiastic parents drag their children about on the end of a leading rein with the mistaken idea that they are implanting in them a love of horses which will never desert them. With girls, it often never does.

Fig. 2. It is not wise to go out and buy a pony and expect the child to climb up and ride it without any practice beforehand

But the same cannot be said for boys. They can so easily be sickened and will gladly exchange the saddle for the machine as soon as they are old enough to assert themselves. Memories of freezing walks on lazy ponies will not encourage him to try again. Nevertheless, he will at least have had a certain amount of pleasure and fresh air and it will, at the same time, have exercised his parent!

So if the child is keen to ride – that is, keen enough that she keeps on asking and will not let the subject drop – then by all means let her begin. But there is absolutely no harm, otherwise, in delaying the start.

It is not wise to go out and buy a pony and then expect the child to climb up and ride it. Riding, like every other worthwhile accomplishment takes a lot of practice before it can be done well. Some young people learn quicker than others, of course, because they are born with natural balance, but everyone must learn the correct aids and how to apply them. Either the child must be taught by a parent who is an experienced horseman or woman or she must go to an establishment and take a course of lessons. It is essential to learn the rudiments, to gain confidence and to acquire a good and natural style of riding without which no rider will ever become expert. A complete novice on a new pony which the family do not know, and, therefore, do not really trust, may end up as the perfect partnership. It equally well may terminate the relationship at an early date with the child's nerve being spoilt for ever.

Some basic first lessons should, therefore, be taken at a reputable School and this applies to the beginner adult quite as much as to the child. The elementary theory of balance may thus be studied and the use of the hands and legs. Various animals can be ridden, because most establishments do not choose to mount beginners on the same pony at each lesson and this will give a valuable insight into the different types of pony. They do vary so much in size and in temperament. Some ponies are very slow and lethargic and need driving on all the time whilst others are quick and responsive.

The old idea of going to a riding school and jogging along a road or lane on a leading rein, until a sufficient modicum of balance and control have been achieved, has now been proved to be less than the ideal. This is still the way some people do it and the end result will be the same in some cases, but not in all. A nervous person, or one to whom natural balance does not come easily, will not find it easy to acquire a good seat and hands without expert teaching.

Some years ago, experts in the equestrian field realised that this was a 'hit or miss' way to learn to ride. It was becoming apparent that there was more to controlling a horse than gripping the saddle with the legs and hanging on by the reins. Riding centres were opened by experts in the art of riding and horsemanship. The whole field of riding and the basic skill needed to do it well, was undergoing a change. It was realised that a beginner would benefit much more by learning in an enclosed area on a well schooled animal. Covered riding schools sprang up like mushrooms. Now the working man or woman is able to take evening riding lessons in winter. These lessons are held by electric light in all weathers. Thus, both parties are gaining. The proprietor does not have his animals standing idle for a large part of the winter months and the school child and the office worker is not restricted to the daylight hours for his riding.

All equestrian centres have outside schooling rings as well so that riding can be enjoyed there in fine weather. Elementary lessons are not given on the leading rein, the instructor is in the centre of the circle unmounted and the beginner's pony is adequately schooled to the work so that the novice is thus able to concentrate, not on controlling his mount so much as perfecting his own skill and balance in the saddle.

This modern trend has done much good in the equestrian world and, as a result of this teaching, we have more good riders about than there have ever been. Moreover, riders are getting much more pleasure out of the sport because they are more skilled at it and the horses and ponies themselves are a great deal more comfortable and responsive.

So if you have an equestrian centre or school in your area go and visit it and, very important, make enquiries about it in the neighbourhood. Past pupils who have learnt there are the people who can best recommend a good school in your area. It is all-important, also, to discover whether the school that you choose is approved by the experts in the horse world. This you can quickly discover by looking for their certificate of official approval which will be prominently displayed or by writing to the British Horse Society, the National Equestrian Centre, Stoneleigh, Kenilworth, Warwickshire. They will send you a booklet which they publish called *Where to Ride*. Every establishment listed in this publication, and two hundred and thirty of them have been approved, will have been visited by one of

Fig. 3. Riding is the building of a partnership and the achieving of harmony between pony and rider

the Society's Qualified Inspectors and there are certain to be one or two, or more, in your area.

There are still, alas, a few disreputable establishments about. They manage to keep going because so many people want to ride. But in too many cases neither riders nor ponies are comfortable and enjoying themselves. There is absolutely no need today for the novice to patronise one of these places. Be quite sure that you learn to ride at an establishment which has been inspected and approved.

In whatever part of the country you may live, you can be sure to find some horsey events to attend. Horse shows and gymkhanas are full of interest for the potential young horseman and there will be lots of knowledgeable people about. Look around before you actually take the big step of embarking upon your riding. Consider carefully the animals that you see at these events and watch how very good some of them have become. These are the horses and ponies which have beeen bred with the right conformation and which have fallen into knowledgeable hands. Your riding centre may not be able to offer many well schooled animals like this, but it will benefit the novice to know what he is striving for and to have in his mind's eye the perfect pony. The right partnership is a pleasure to watch in action. This will take many months and years of hard work for you to achieve but there is absolutely no reason why you should not get there in the end. Riding is the building of a partnership and the achieving of harmony between pony and rider. When this ideal state of affairs has been reached, riding, and caring for your horse, will have become one of your most exciting and enjoyable experiences.

CHAPTER TWO

EXPLORING RIDING FACILITIES IN THE AREA AND THE ADVANTAGES OF THE RIDING SCHOOL SYSTEM OF LIVERY

When you start riding you will be ignorant of the basic practices of looking after a pony. Before you can sit in the saddle, gather up the reins and move off, you will have to catch the animal, feed him, groom him and saddle up. A pony is not like a bicycle which can be propped up against the wall when finished with and which requires the minimum of maintenance. There are not very many ponies which will not object to a novice handling him entirely. Inexpert hands dragging bridles over their ears and eyes and fumbling hands drawing up girth straps can be irritating to a young well-schooled pony. An old stolid pony will probably accept the situation with resignation but he may not be a good type for you to learn on. These ponies give confidence but are generally unresponsive to the aids and dull to ride. Teaching yourself can be a very slow process and you may pick up faults of style which become gradually worse if they are not corrected at an early stage. The more you practise with an incorrect leg position and a bad seat, the harder it will be to correct these habits later.

So it is clear from the above that the beginner without an experienced parent or friend to guide him in the first stages of his riding, will be wise to go to a school of riding. Every child and young adult, anyway, will be working, either at school, college or in a job. Thus evenings and week-ends are the only time he, or she, will have free to ride and the pony will be left very much alone. Arrange to have a lesson once a week for three months. At the end of this period a certain basic skill will have been achieved and you will know whether you wish to continue with the sport. After this, another three months riding on a slightly more advanced level will still be necessary before you should think of becoming an owner yourself.

Try to find a riding school where you will be allowed to help with grooming, tack cleaning and general care of the horses. Many schools encourage their pupils in this and it helps tremendously to give beginners a feel for horses. They will become accustomed to their ways. If you can become efficient and reliable at looking after a pony and have, unfortunately, no hope of owning one yourself, you may find yourself acting as temporary owner while a pony-owning friend has a holiday. Quite a lot of people are on the look out for someone to exercise, or care for their pony for these periods. Whatever your prospects, learn as much as you possibly can during that first six months.

What is the weekly lesson going to cost the beginner? A very important consideration. Children are generally charged 40p to 50p a half hour for a lesson and 62½p for a whole hour. Adults will be slightly more, 62½p to 75p for a half hour and £1.05 an hour for individual instruction.* Although individual instruction costs more, for an adult, especially, it is well worth it.

Beginners are not taken into open fields because of the difficulty of opening gates and controlling the horses. Avoid a school which takes complete novices out for rides. Teaching may be adequate but it is just as likely to be non-existent. Lessons in an enclosed schooling area will be much more beneficial. Progress is bound to be slow at the beginning but after the first six lessons the basic skill will be acquired and you should be starting to achieve the 'rise' at the trot. This is a big step in the ladder and your riding will be correspondingly much more comfortable when you have achieved it. The pace will gradually quicken, your mount will appreciate that his rider is beginning to master the rudiments of riding and he will respond more readily and easily. The first foundations are being laid for that perfect

* These figures recorded in 1970.

17

partnership between pony and rider which we are going to achieve in due course.

During this basic six months whilst we are enjoying our lessons at the riding school, if the next plan is to become the proud possessor of our own pony this must be given careful thought meanwhile. Consider how much time you will have to give to the animal.

During the winter the pony must be fed and watered regularly and all the year round it must be kept clean and healthy. Remember those dark mornings before school or college. Will you feel like going out to the field and giving him his breakfast? Or, even more time-taking, will you feel like mucking out his stable before you get your own breakfast? If you are at boarding-school someone else will have the job to do but if you are at home it will be your responsibility. Visiting the pony twice a day might become tedious, but it must be done. Not only your pony, but his stable and his tack must be kept clean. A clean healthy pony in a dirty bridle will not look right. He will also appreciate your company, as much as you can spare of it, if he lives alone, because ponies are very gregarious and most of them like to be visited.

You are the pony's master and friend and you are responsible for his well-being. If by any mischance he should fall ill, you must do everything possible to get him well again, for he can do nothing to help himself. Sick ponies, alas, can be rather expensive luxuries but we hope such misfortunes will not befall you and yours. Nevertheless, these matters must be most carefully considered beforehand.

Any pony worth its salt who is going to give its owner a good ride must be kept fairly regularly exercised. Otherwise, he will become soft and lazy or, just as likely, naughty and unco-operative. Many winter days are not very conducive to riding but the job will have to be done in bad weather as well as in fair.

This all sounds very discouraging but it is much better to look at the job with a clear understanding of what you are embarking upon when you wish to learn to ride and to become a horse owner. In fact, lots and lots of young people not only think it is worth the hard work involved, they love the job. There is no more rewarding companion than a pony and the fun and pleasure he brings you will amply repay the time and money you must give up to looking after him. There really is a satisfaction in getting out into the fresh air every morning before work. All over the country children and young people are riding their ponies at week-ends and in the evenings in all weathers and getting much pleasure from it. So there must be something very worthwhile about this riding business or they wouldn't be doing it.

Consider carefully what your local facilities are for riding in the area. Have you common land, bridle paths and friendly farmers nearby, or are you encircled by busy main roads? Never ride over any farmer's land without visiting him first and obtaining his permission. Maps are now available with rights of ways and bridle paths marked on them and these are very useful for the horseman.

Having obtained permission you must be very considerate of the farmer's land. Do not gallop over his fields especially when the ground is wet, and always shut every gate, leaving it exactly as you found it. Stock should not be disturbed. If a flock of sheep is grazing in a field, do your best not to set them running.

If you live in a built up area, however, and the roads are very busy then your problem is, alas, a serious one. The highways today are very dangerous for ponies. Fatal accidents are not unknown. Under these circumstances it might be more sensible for you to keep your pony at the riding school. This is a very popular scheme today and more and more horselovers are taking advantage of the facilities offered by the proprietors of these schools.

Basically, the idea is for the owner to buy a pony and hand it over to the riding school to keep for her 'at livery'. If arrangements are made for the school to use the pony for lessons and rides for their pupils during the week, the cost will thus be halved and the pony will be kept well exercised. The owner, of course, rides him herself when she has time and has priority over the other riders. She will also be welcome to help care for him, clean his tack and take him out alone when she wishes.

This arrangement, with variations, is obviously a very sensible one for the horselover who does not have a lot of time for exercising and looking after her pony and who may live in an unattractive area for riding. She will be glad to make use of the establishment's schooling area, or ménage as it is called, and she will have company for her rides and for doing the pony chores.

The school will gain the use of a pony for its pupils and in most cases are quite willing to discuss arrangements to suit both parties. This method of keeping a pony should cost about £3 to £4 a week. Full livery, where the pony is not used by other visitors to the school, will probably be nearly double this amount so you see there is no wonder it is such a popular scheme.

A novice would obviously be well-advised to consider this arrangement. She could do this for several years and should at the end of this period have acquired a good working knowledge of pony management and be much better qualified to look after a horse, which it will probably have to be by this time, should she now wish to tackle the job single-handed.

There will probably be several riding establishments in your area which are recommended by the British Horse Society. Visit them all, a good school will not mind enquiries. Look at the horses and their premises and their equipment and watch the staff at work. Small, humble buildings will not necessarily mean uncared for ponies. Make it quite clear that you are a novice yourself, but a serious minded one who will become a regular pupil as soon as a satisfactory school can be found.

CHAPTER THREE

FINDING THE RIGHT PONY

The decision to buy a pony having been reached, and arrangements made as to where, and how, it is to be kept, the next thing to be done is to find the right animal.

The rider will not, we hope, by this time, be a complete novice, if she has followed the advice laid down in the first two chapters. We hope she will have had some lessons and will have learnt the rudiments of the sport. She will, also, have considered whether she has enough money, first, to buy the pony and then, to keep it.

We have considered how much it should cost to keep the pony but it is not so easy to give an exact figure for buying the animal. A pony can cost anything between £50 and £150, or more.

A well-broken sensible pony which can be easily handled by a child and which will go willingly for her in traffic and in open country is what we are looking for. Such a paragon is also what a lot of other people want. Of course a lot of good ponies change hands from family to family without ever being advertised or taken to public sales. As they are outgrown, so they are sold to friends who know their worth. But pony breeding has now become a fashionable pastime and pony studs are flourishing all over the country. The supply is beginning at last to catch up with the demand and breeders are endeavouring to produce the right type of animal and to school it adequately to meet present day requirements. The latter, of course, is the most difficult thing to achieve. It is easy enough to send a pony to stud, it is delightful when the foal is born but as it grows to maturity and needs expert schooling to turn it into a safe mount for a child, so a problem arises. There are not enough skilled horse trainers about. So beware the very young half-broken pony. He is not for you.

You have probably heard of auction sales and may, in fact, have attended one of these fascinating events. They are full of interest for the horselover and you will have a delightful day watching the horses and ponies, assessing their qualities and conjuring up happy visions of bidding for and buying several of them to take home. But this you must firmly resist doing, in reality! Although a few good ponies are sold under the hammer in this way, they are comparatively rare and there are far more useless animals than genuine ones disposed of like this. Many of them have something basically wrong and this will only be discernible to a really knowledgeable person. Moreover, they may not be safe to ride on a highway or may possess a vice which will not be apparent at the auction sale.

Study the advertisements in the equine journals and the local press. They make interesting reading and many of them will sound ideal. In fact, if all the horses advertised were the paragons of virtue that their owners describe them to be, we should have no difficulty in finding the perfect pony. An advertisement may be misleading, however, and it would be unwise to buy a pony through an advertisement without first seeing and trying it. Nevertheless, the columns of advertisements can teach quite a lot. An idea of the average price of ponies in the district will be gained and descriptions given are interesting. The price will fluctuate very much and will be governed by various factors – breeding, age, temperament and performance.

Never buy a pony through an advertisement without first trying it. Preferably arrange to have it on trial, but a lot of owners and breeders are not keen to allow this now. A great pity for those who are genuine buyers, but understandable from the owner's point of view. Even a good pony can be spoilt by careless handling in a week and accidents can happen.

The usual arrangement now, is to go over and try the

pony at the stable where he is being sold. You will be allowed to try him at all paces and to jump if you wish. Take an experienced friend with you. The riding master or mistress, or one of the head stable girls from the riding school you have been attending would probably be the right person. If you are to be allowed the pony on trial for a few days then make the most of this time. You want to find out if he is quiet to ride, but not too sluggish, quiet to handle and groom, unperturbed by traffic and easy to catch. This last point is very important. When an hour is set aside for riding it is extremely frustrating to have to spend most of that time coaxing the pony to come to you and have his halter put on. Ponies which are bad to catch are generally worse in the summer months anyway, and this is exactly when you will be wanting to make most use of him.

You may be advised by friends not to go to a dealer on any account. They seem to have made a reputation for themselves of being rogues, an untrustworthy lot who will sell you an unsound nag in disguise for a good one. To a certain extent this is a false impression, although it probably was true of a number of dealers fifty years ago.

Remember that a horse dealer has to live by his reputation and he does not really want to get a name for selling poor quality animals. Sooner or later he will become known for this and will lose in the end.

Some dealers have horsemen coming back to them over and over again because they have proved reliable in supplying good, sound horses. This applies chiefly, of course, to a man or woman who likes to buy a new hunter every year. Yes, there really are people who can still afford to do this! These dealers will take a horse or pony back if it proves unsuitable and will try to find you another. If you decide to try and buy through a dealer, go to a man who has been well recommended, tell him how much experience you have had and how much you are prepared to pay for the pony.

Do not be too disheartened if you try several ponies over a long period and none of them proves quite suitable. Your pony will turn up in the end. Much better to be cautious and to wait until you find the right one, than to spend £120 on an animal which frightens you or which you will grow out of in six months' time. It is a funny thing, anyway, that horses and ponies are easier to buy than to sell. But very likely the same could be said about buying and selling a car or a dog.

The normal procedure, when you at last do find a pony to suit you, is to have the veterinary surgeon examine him before he changes hands for cash. He will thoroughly check the animal to be sure that he is sound in wind, limb, and eye and the usual charge for this service is £3.15. But it is well worth it so do not try to economise by omitting this examination. If the pony is bought at a sale or through an advertisement and carries already a veterinary certificate of soundness, be quite sure to check the date that the certificate was issued.

CHAPTER FOUR

THE PONY BREEDS

It is interesting for the beginner to look at the different breeds of ponies in Britain today, because we have such a wonderful inheritance in this sphere. Our native ponies are now world famous and are being exported all over the world. Anyone embarking upon riding as a new interest, or, considering buying a pony themselves, should know something about them.

The variety of breeds and pony characteristics must be confusing to the novice. Study the photographs in the magazines devoted to the horse and his welfare. Excellent examples of the different breeds appear at frequent intervals. Then, when you visit a show you will be able to pick out the different types and breeds for yourself.

The National Pony Society, and the Ponies of Great Britain Club, both hold first class fixtures in different parts of the country. These are well-organised shows with beautiful ponies being shown both in-hand and under saddle, a shop window for the general public. Interested spectators may talk to the breeders and owners, inspect the ponies and decide from these visits which is the type of pony they feel will best fit their own requirements.

There is a flourishing export trade in ponies from Britain and prospective buyers now come from all over the world. More than a thousand registered ponies are exported annually. Each breed has its own society which aims to foster interest in their chosen breed, and these societies are supported by a band of enthusiasts. These ponies have now become big business and the National Pony Society is the parent organisation. It is the oldest society of its kind in the world and the committee are knowledgeable people whose experience and expert advice are of great value to the scores of small breeders all over the country. The National Pony Society publishes a stud book and a register of polo and riding ponies, it organises an annual sale of ponies of all breeds and ages and also stages a two-day show for all the native breeds, polo ponies and thoroughbred riding ponies.

Probably the ponies we see most of in the show ring come from Wales. They are very good-looking and are most popular with breeders because their qualities are such that they do catch the public eye. Roughly, these ponies can be divided into two groups, the Welsh ponies of riding type and the Welsh Mountain pony. The latter are very pretty and resemble the Arab horse in miniature, with the same attractive head carriage and concave profile, the large dark eye and the fine muzzle. They do not exceed 12 hands in height (a 'hand' measures 4 inches) and are predominantly grey, but there are also chestnuts and bays to be found.

For generations these ponies have roamed the Welsh hills, as do other native breeds which I shall describe, and the very first record of them was found to be in 1138. Approved stallions are granted premiums annually to run with the mares on the hills. It is delightful to see the herds on the grassy Welsh slopes, grazing peacefully in idyllic surroundings.

The Welsh pony of riding type may reach 13.2 hands in height. Basically it closely resembles its cousin, with the same beautiful head, true straight action and typical pony character. They are frequently in the ribbons in the show ring. As riding ponies they are splendid, on condition that they have been carefully broken and well handled thereafter. Keen, fast, lively ponies, they are not for the complete beginner, at least until they have matured and provided they have always been well ridden.

It may be that devotees of the breed will not agree with the statement that these Welsh ponies are not suitable for novice riders. Possibly this may be true for a few of them who are quiet and kind. But, on the whole, the Welsh pony should be regarded as a child's second pony and not as a novice child's mount.

In the north-east corner of Devon is an attractive moorland area known as Exmoor, and here we find herds of small ponies. These animals have been saved from extinction by a group of enthusiastic supporters who recognised the sterling qualities of the breed and work very hard to preserve them. These Exmoor ponies are delightful companions for beginners. Intelligent, and full of 'pony' sense, and character, they make reliable mounts for children and excellent children's hunters.

Supporters of the Exmoor pony believe it to be the hardiest pony breed in the world. They do provide good foundation stock for breeding and it is a fact that at least one Grand National Winner sprang from Exmoor stock.

These ponies average 12 to 13 hands in height and are usually dark brown or bay in colour. The breed is characterised by the 'mealy' or light biscuit colour of the muzzle. During winter months the pony's coat grows thick and harsh and carries very little bloom. Undoubtedly this is due to generations past when the herds had to survive on the moors without food or shelter.

Today, breeders concern themselves actively with the welfare of the herds and they are given winter rations and regularly looked over. Every year a number are lost on the roads, killed by passing motorists which annually become a greater hazard to their welfare. Driving over Exmoor some months ago, looking for these native ponies in a thick mist, we appreciated that although the motorist is blamed for these sad fatalities it may not always be entirely his fault. We were travelling at 10 m.p.h. but we still narrowly missed decapitating a foal who lay unconcerned on the grass verge with hooves and head actually on the tarmac. The mare was grazing the sweet short grass which grew on the verge. In the mist, it was impossible to discern them, until almost too late. Having become accustomed to traffic they do not trouble to move out of the way, particularly when fog obscures visibility and deadens engine noise.

Pony sales are held annually at Bampton, near Dulverton. The registered herds are rounded up and the yearlings or 'suckers', as they are called, are inspected and duly registered. It is quite possible for the knowledgeable horseman to buy a young unbroken pony at one of these sales for £20 or £30 and this is a good bargain for the man who can school his own novice pony. The beginner should beware, however, breaking in youngsters is not yet for him, or her.

Dartmoor ponies are smaller than their cousins on Exmoor but their lives are fundamentally the same. They have been bred for centuries on the high moorland terrain of Dartmoor which stands over 1,000 feet. They are extremely hardy, sure-footed and active little ponies with delightful temperaments. Many breeders of these ponies do not allow their registered animals to roam loose now, however, because as on Exmoor, there is risk of losing them on the roads.

In late autumn, sales are held at Okehampton, Hatherleigh, Tavistock, Chagford and Ashburton. On investigation, however, we found many of these ponies to be unregistered and the same situation will appertain on Exmoor.

Brown, bay or black are the Dartmoor ponies' true colours. White markings are allowed, particularly a small star on the forehead. No white at all is permitted on a registered Exmoor. Inspecting the herds of ponies running on the moors, we were surprised to see how many coloured ponies there were. There were piebald and skewbald animals in every group. Throwbacks, possibly, to gipsy mares, but this colour is prevalent amongst the unregistered wild ponies living in a semi-feral state.

Membership of the Dartmoor Pony Society is increasing and there is now an attractive new showground for the breed at Brimpts Farm, Dartmeet in the very heart of Dartmoor. Well-broken registered Dartmoor ponies are much in demand and make splendid mounts for young children and beginners.

The largest of the native pony breeds, of true riding type, is the New Forest pony. They make splendid family ponies as they stand from 12 hands to 14.2 hands high and have delightful, kind temperaments. Alas, these ponies suffered severely from outside crosses and they are not so distinctive in type and colour as their smaller brethren on Exmoor and Dartmoor. The last thirty years, however, has seen a tremendous improvement, and the New Forest Pony Breeding Society report now that no outcrosses take place in the Forest. The ponies have been recognised in the area from ancient times and Canute's law of the Royal Forest, proclaimed at Winchester in 1016, mentions large numbers of wild horses, cattle and even buffaloes, roaming at large.

Building and industrial development has now reduced the land available for running herds. The breed continues, nevertheless, to flourish and sales are held, generally in August, September or early October near Beaulieu in Hampshire. Buyers come from all over England as well as overseas.

These ponies are not so nervous as the Exmoor and Dartmoor ponies and have become quite a nuisance to visitors driving through the Forest area. They peer inquisitively into the litter bins and help themselves. They have docile natures and are ideal mounts for young people. They will go hunting, perform at gymkhanas and can even be trained to polo or to harness. A better all-round pony would be hard to find. The New Forest fits the bill for many young riders.

These ponies come in a variety of colours, bay being, I think, predominant but chestnuts, greys and browns are common. They have lovely shoulders, are deep through the girth and display a free graceful action. The ponies' heads tend to be rather large in many cases but this is not necessarily unattractive.

The Shetland pony must be known to even the most inexperienced beginner in the horse world. They are the smallest representatives of the native ponies of the British Isles and they come from the Shetland Isles where they

29

Fig. 4. Shetland pony

lived a nomadic life for many years before being brought over to the mainland. It was interesting to discover, when conducting research into the breed for the purposes of this book, that, apparently, the Viking warriors were so impressed by the ponies on the Islands of the north-east coast of Scotland that they named the region 'Hrossey' meaning, Horse Island.

These small animals lived a precarious life on the Islands before being brought over to the mainland. They are tiny, standing only 9 hands to 11 hands high but are immensely strong and hardy for their size. They grow profuse manes and tails and long thick coats in winter. Their intelligence is far in excess of their miniature stature. They are, in many cases, far too clever and quick thinking for a beginner. Lovable and attractive they may be, but naughty as well. Of course, as with every breed, there are exceptions, and if a Shetland has been well schooled from its earliest formative years and carefully ridden, he may become a delightful pet and be perfectly safe for a child. But too many of them are more suited to leading-rein riding and harness work. The deep strong girth and sturdy build make them good driving ponies but with our highways so congested this delightful form of transport is not for a beginner.

The older novice rider would be well advised to consider a

Fell pony. These ponies originate from Northumberland, Cumberland and Westmorland and, although of a docile nature, are up to a lot of weight. They are most useful for pony-trekking centres, being very sure-footed and capable of carrying father, mother or daughter. But not all three together!

The Fell stands up to 14 hands in height, is always black or dark brown and rejoices in a luxurious flowing mane and tail. His temperament is gentle and kind but despite his heavy build he is not at all sluggish. He has a good free stride and an enthusiasm for company and for exercise. A small herd of registered Fell pony mares is still turned out each year on Shap Fell and, also at Caldbeck, and a registered champion stallion runs with them.

In Northumberland several farmers keep Fell ponies for riding round their sheep. Others in the district are kept for riding and hunting.

Highland ponies are also called Garrons and were originally used to carry grouse and deer from the hill in the shooting season. Some are still used for this purpose. These ponies are predominantly grey or dun in colour, the latter having a black stripe along the back which has become a distinctive feature of the breed. They are quite large, up to 14.2 hands in height and inclined to be broad for a novice. Nevertheless, they are sensible, intelligent ponies and an economical proposition for the family who want a pony which every member can ride. Trekking establishments are full of them, like their Fell brethren, they are sure-footed and suited to the type of terrain over which these establishments like to take their visitors.

One of the oldest breeds known in Great Britain and, deservedly, one of the most popular, is the Connemara pony from Ireland. These are lovely ponies, usually grey in colour and admirably suited to the older novice beginner. Height varies between 13 hands and 14.2 hands and some of these animals are very nice looking and much in demand as breeding stock.

31

It is legend that the rich Galway merchants of several hundred years ago imported some fine Arab horses, some of which are reputed to have escaped and joined local herds of ponies running wild on the mountains. So the Connemara pony, as we know it today, was evolved.

The English Connemara Pony Society will help beginners to find a good specimen of the breed and are actively concerned with importing only the best type of pony to England.

These notes should act as a guide in the beginner's search for her ideal pony. Not every pony you see will be a pure-bred native but it is immensely valuable to study the right type and to have this picture in mind.

Having explored the different breeds and decided that one of these native pure-bred animals is the ideal, how much are you going to have to pay for one? This, in many cases, will be a deciding factor. These lovely ponies are expensive. The breeder has had to nurture the pony from infancy, school it expertly to bring it to riding perfection, and she is not going to sell it for less than £150, at the least. This is the absolute minimum that you will have to pay for a native five-year-old schooled pony.

What of the other ponies that we see all over the countryside, carrying youngsters hunting, showing and pony clubbing? They are not all specimens of our lovely native ponies. These are crossbred ponies of every type, size and colour many of them having originally derived from pure bred ponies. It is becoming increasingly popular now to breed a foal from one's favourite mare, regardless of whether she is the right type to perpetuate her stock.

Knowledgeable breeders are aiming at a quality pony, of equable temperament and gentle disposition. A pony which is free moving and willing, but easily controlled by the weak muscles of the novice rider. First cross ponies, from native pony mares and thoroughbred stallions make lovely mounts. But novice owners must beware the semi-thoroughbred ponies. These animals go well in experienced hands, responsive to hand and leg aids and with delightful action, making a ride a joy for the owner. But our beginner's pony will very likely have to live outside for a good part of the year, if not all of it, and she will be occupied with other responsibilities in her life than looking after her pony. Ponies in most families are often subject to enforced idleness for several months and then experience bursts of great activity during school and college holidays. This sort of life a native pony will cope with, and he will adapt himself to the change, but a thoroughbred pony would suffer some deprivation, loss of condition and a deterioration in manners.

Depending upon the size of pony our beginner needs to carry him, it is, therefore, wise to allow at least £100 with which to buy him. Probably more will be necessary, but you might be lucky and find a good cross-bred pony, outgrown by a family, or in a riding school, and for sale at around £80.

Do not be too definite about not paying more than a specific amount for your pony. A good one is worth his weight in gold and will repay the initial outlay many times.

CHAPTER FIVE

EQUIPMENT NECESSARY FOR THE RIDER AND THE PONY

Whether the novice is going to aspire to buying a pony of her own, or is going to stick to riding at a school or equitation centre, without the responsibility of ownership, she will require some basic equipment for herself.

What exactly does she need, where to buy it and how much to pay?

There are one or two necessities in the rider's wardrobe. The full regalia will only become necessary when she makes her debut in the hunting field or the show ring. Until then, buy a hard velvet riding cap. This is the most important item on the list. It is a safety precaution as well as an essential bit of riding equipment. It will cost about £4 and is available at all stores which stock riding garments. A good place to buy one may be on one of the stands at your local agricultural show. We purchase a lot of equipment in this way and save many shopping expeditions. Never buy a riding hat without first trying it on, one's head is a very individual thing, and the hat being made of hard material, it is not pliable, and the sizing given may not match up to the recipient's shape of head. They are very uncomfortable things to wear if they do not fit properly. The rider's comfort and safety may depend upon a good fit. This hat must always be worn for riding.

One pair of jodhpurs is the next necessity. Two, if you can afford it. Novice riders can be seen at riding schools riding in jeans but they are not very comfortable. Discard them as soon as you can afford jodhpurs. New ones will cost £5 or £6, or more depending on whether you are child or adult size. Adult jodhpurs will cost £9 or £10. Stretchy ones are very popular and look smart but are not very warm for winter wear and are usually made in a light biscuit colour which quickly gets dirty if you have to do your own stable work. Buy corded or thick twill jodhpurs and they should last a long while and survive a good bit of wear and tear. All jodhpurs are made, today, in materials which will stand being put in the family washing machine.

With these two basic pieces of equipment you can go anywhere on a pony. Anoraks and school burberrys, and walking shoes, will not look elegant, but they will be adequate, and you can become just as good a rider in them as the person who is turned out to perfection.

The next thing to purchase would be a tweed jacket. Not an essential, but how much nicer than the anorak it will look. Choose one in a heather mixture or a small check. A boy rider will find it most useful for other activities besides his riding. It will be adequately cleaned by being given a good brush the evening before a special occasion. A new tweed jacket will cost £10 to £15, so try and get one second-hand.

A polo-necked jersey looks very nice under a tweed jacket, particularly a yellow one. Everyone can find this type of jersey today or persuade someone to make one. Gloves should be made of string, not wool, and are usually made in yellow or light fawn. Not very practical, as they get dirty so quickly. Woollen gloves make it awkward to handle the reins when they are wet.

The expense of jodhpur boots might be justified if you are going to do a lot of riding. Girls, especially, love them and say that they are more comfortable than ordinary shoes to ride in. We never had them as children so I cannot consider them essential. We did very well without them, and still do. They do, however, look very smart and pleasing. They will cost around £5, more, or less, according to size.

A mackintosh, of sorts, is very necessary, in this climate, unless most of the riding is going to be confined to lessons in a covered riding school. A lightweight plastic one will not do. Proper riding mackintoshes are desirable for hunting but new ones are expensive, about £15 to £20. They are also remarkably difficult to clean efficiently, which is tiresome because they are always produced in a light fawn colour. They are more comfortable to ride in than an ordinary mackintosh because they are specially made with a good slit up the back so that the sides sit well over the saddle and the pony's loins.

A riding cane may be regarded as a part of the wardrobe. Most people find them useful once they have learnt how to handle one as well as the reins. Leather ones cost £2 or £3. Hunting whips, with a thong and a lash, are quite unnecessary, and the desire to possess one must be firmly resisted.

Remember when buying riding clothes that good quality garments will last longer and this is important if there are younger members of the family to whom the things will come down. Keep them as clean and well-brushed as possible, an untidy rider is a discredit to her mount.

Many Pony Club branches now run a second-hand riding kit service and so it is worthwhile investigating the possibility in your area. Serviceable out-grown riding clothes change hands sometimes once or twice.

The rider being now suitably attired, the next step, if she is lucky enough to have her own pony, or has the prospect of doing so, is to fit the animal out with 'tack', which is the correct term for saddle and bridle.

Some ponies are sold complete with tack, but if this is so in your case, take the precaution of carefully checking the saddle and bridle. Or, better still, ask your expert friend who has helped you choose the pony, to do so. Some people who sell ponies find this a convenient way of adding a little more to the price of the animal and getting rid of worn-out tack. Leather does not last for ever, check the eye holes at the buckles on the bridles, these may be very worn. Make sure that girths are not worn out and the stuffing not spilling out

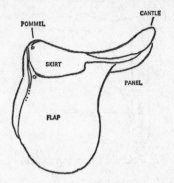

Fig. 5. Saddle

of the saddle. Poor quality tack, which has been neglected, is uneconomical and can be a potential cause of accidents. Dry brittle leather is liable to break at crucial moments.

A good saddle is expensive so if we are going to buy one, we shall need to take care of it. Far better buy a good quality second-hand saddle and many saddlers have excellent ones for sale. A new one will cost £20 or £30. There is now a lovely child's saddle especially designed to specifications laid down by the Pony Club and selling at around £21·25.

The fitting of the saddle is important. The front arch

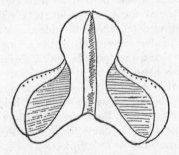

Fig. 6. Correct way to lay down saddle

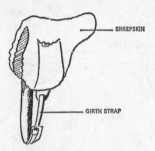

Fig. 7. Child's numnah saddle

should clear the pony's withers by the breadth of not less than two fingers when the rider is mounted. The girths should come three or four inches behind the point of the elbow. Felt saddles are useful for very small children. They are comfortable for child and pony and are cheaper to buy than leather saddles. Beware of a saddle of this type, however, for the older child. They do collect moths and must be regularly checked for deterioration.

Every saddle should have safety bars to which the stirrup leathers are fastened, these are to be found under the small leather flaps on each side of the saddle. Check that they are not stiff or rusty. The stirrup irons should not be too small for the feet, there should be half an inch clearance at the side of the shoe at the widest point to avoid the risk of the foot getting wedged, should the rider have a fall. Safety stirrups are a modern invention for the young rider. They have a rubber band on one side which should be on the outside and this band falls off if any pressure is placed on it so that the risk of the foot being caught is negligible.

Today there is such a wide variety of bridles used for ponies that it is confusing for a novice to know what is best. The leather parts are the same for any bridle, it is the bit which differs, the bit is the mouthpiece.

The bit is a means of telling the pony what his rider wants him to do. It must, therefore, fit comfortably in the

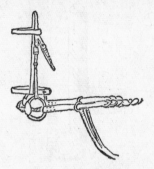

Fig. 8. Snaffle bridle

pony's mouth and not be drawn up too high or hang too low
so that he nibbles and chews it with his teeth.

The snaffle bit is the more satisfactory for the beginner
and any pony she is likely to buy should go kindly in one.
This is a jointed bar with two large rings at the sides which
fasten to the leather cheek pieces. There is only one rein
and this is easy to fit and to keep clean. Double bridles and
pelham bridles are not for the novice, they are more severe
than a snaffle and popular for showing or for stopping strong
ponies out hunting. A snaffle bridle, for a pony, will cost

SNAFFLE
CURB

Fig. 9. Double bridle

Fig. 10. Hemp halter

around £10 new but you might easily get one second-hand for £6 or £7.

Ponies which throw up their heads constantly may need to wear martingales but the average pony will not need one. The standing martingale goes from the noseband to the girth and has a strap around the neck, the pony's neck, not the rider's. This strap around the neck is very useful for the novices to hold on to, however, when jumping, so if the pony at the riding school where you learn happens to be wearing one, make use of it in emergencies.

The above is the essential tack used for riding. The pony will also need a halter or headcollar. A halter made of hemp will only cost £1 and will do quite well for a quiet pony. It will be used for leading the pony in and out of his field and for tying him up when he is being groomed. A headcollar is more elaborate, and expensive, being similar to the headpiece of a bridle without the bit. It is useful for a pony to wear if he is difficult to catch but novice riders do not want to start by owning ponies that are awkward to catch and so a halter should do quite adequately as a start.

Equipment for the care of the pony can be kept to a few simple necessities. But these items should be gathered together before the pony arrives. Two buckets will be needed, one for watering the pony and one for cleaning tack.

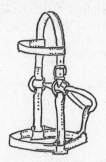

Fig. 11. Headcollar

Wooden ones are lovely and look very professional as well as being less likely to be knocked over, but metal ones from any hardware store will do quite well. Haynets cost about £1 each and two are useful for the busy owner who can fill them both in the morning and save time after work in the evening, or vice versa. They can be used in the field quite as well as the stable and prevent the hay being blown about or trampled in the mud. It is very important that they are tied securely and high, so there is no danger of the pony getting its foot caught in the mesh.

A large shovel, a brush and a fork for handling straw will be needed if the pony is to be in the stable at all. A barrow will be useful but there is sure to be one in the garden shed you can borrow. If not, then tear an old sack in half and use this for collecting the droppings.

Grooming kit consists basically of a dandy brush, curry comb, tail comb, hoof pick, body-brush, and a stable rubber, which is just like a kitchen drying towel. How, and when, to use these items will be discussed in the next chapter. Each of the above items will cost about 50p and it is not wise to buy the child's size as they are soon outgrown.

The above are all the essentials for the care and comfort of the beginner's pony. If he is a hardy native it is not even essential to have a stable. It may all sound like an expensive outlay but there should be no need to replace anything for many years, if good quality items are purchased. Anyway, a pony kept at a riding school will not need as much as the pony kept by itself at home.

CHAPTER SIX

FEEDING AND GENERAL CARE OF THE PONY

How much looking after the pony will need will necessarily depend upon whether he is kept at a riding school or at home. If the riding school plan is adopted, and I cannot stress the value of this idea too highly for the beginner, provided the school is a good one and terms are not prohibitive, then you will be able to learn from the staff at the riding establishment. But if you have a field at home and can afford time to look after and exercise the animal all by yourself, then it is time to consider what the routine of looking after him is going to entail.

A common mistake many novice riders make is to ask a neighbouring farmer to allow their pony to graze in one of his large pastures. This is splendid during winter months so long as the field is not too far away for the extra feeding during bad weather conditions that will be necessary. But what happens when the spring brings the new grass? The pony gets fatter and fatter and within a month he has foundered. This means that laminitis has been contracted due to over-eating. The sensitive layers underneath the wall of the foot become inflamed and the pony can hardly walk. The condition does respond to treatment by the veterinary surgeon but it is a slow process and necessitates keeping the pony off grass for the best part of the day, curtails riding and is expensive.

So beware the large lush pasture which looks so tempting. Leave it to the cows and try and find something more modest. The pony will be fitter and healthier in the long run. An average charge for running a pony in a field would be 50p to 75p a week, more in some areas. Farmers do not care much for having ponies on their land, anyway, because they are a nuisance when stock are being moved from field to

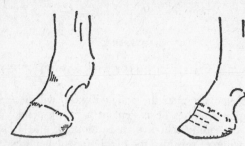

Fig. 12. Normal pony foot – and appearance of foot following laminitis

field and horses do not improve the quality of grass. Land can become horse-sick owing to the tendency for horses to graze, and move on, and to neglect coarse grasses, so that a patchy growth is encouraged. They also tend to leave their droppings amongst the coarse grasses which quickly sours the area.

Probably, if the decision has been reached to keep the pony yourself then you will have suitable premises on which it may graze. Let us hope so, because it will be cheaper for you, and much nicer too. But do remember in spring or summer if the paddock is a large one, that any tendency to laminitis must be watched for. It will not be necessary to ask an expert – anyone who has had much to do with ponies will know the signs. At the first hint of trouble you must tether him during the day or stable him at night, whichever is easiest.

Water in the field will be necessary. A source of running water is ideal, but otherwise an old tank or bath will do quite well, provided it is kept clean and filled with fresh water. A shed for shelter and for feeding, is useful, but not essential. Some ponies do not take advantage of shelter when it is offered, anyway, as they seem to prefer to be out in all weathers. It is important to check the fences too, because loose or sagging wire is dangerous and as the craft of fencing seems to be a dying art many paddocks have weak and

Fig. 13. Broken fences are a potential hazard

patched-up places. Old tins, bottles and any other rubbish that you find should be picked up before the pony occupies the field.

If our beginner is fortunate enough to own a stable at home, this can be put ready, as it will be most useful whilst the interesting business of grooming and saddling up takes place. It is not likely that any first pony she will have will need stabling all the time, this means a lot of work and we can safely leave it to the owner of thoroughbred ponies and those which are regularly ridden and kept at riding schools.

Persuade the handyman in the family to put up some pegs in the stable. They will come in useful for a variety of purposes. The saddle, the bridle, the grooming kit bag and halter will all need hanging up.

During mild weather the pony will not need any extra feeding provided the field is a reasonable size. An overgrown tennis court, by the way, will not do. It is surprising, and very sad, that some ignorant people think it will, with consequent severe deprivation to the unfortunate pony.

When colder weather comes, particularly frost and snow, a good supply of hay will have been laid in and several sacks of pony cubes bought.

Hay will provide the pony with sufficient nourishment under normal winter conditions. This is, of course, dried grass and it should be bought as 'old' hay, that is, it should be at least one year old and not be 'new'. Good meadow hay rustles when it is shaken up and has a yellow colour and a sweet smell. Do not buy musty, mildewed hay with a lot of thistle and weed in it.

When you buy the hay it will be packed tight in bales. Break a chunk off the bale when you feed the pony, but be sure you shake it out well before packing it into the haynet or wooden sack. Hay provides the bulk that the pony needs to make up for the lack of grass.

Concentrates are oats, bran and pony cubes. Oats must be firmly resisted by our beginner at all costs. Leave them to the thoroughbreds and the ponies during regular hard work. Oats have an unfortunate effect on the average child's pony which will turn awkward on a pound a day very quickly. The feeding situation for ponies has been revolutionised by the production of a most valuable and nutritious form of food called horse and pony cubes. Adult horses thrive on them as well, but, be sure to ask for pony cubes for our animal. They cost about £2 a bag but this will last a long while, at least six weeks. They are worth every penny, anyway, because they are admirable feeding value and never 'hot' the pony up, like oats will. A pound a day during frost and snow is sufficient for the average pony, and pony cubes you can buy at any fodder merchants.

Ponies do love turnips, apples and carrots as well but these can be kept as a luxury and only bought when pocket money funds allow.

Feeding and care of the pony will not be easy for a beginner who must learn by experience when her pony is looking poor and needing more nutritious food and when he is becoming too fat from over-feeding. Call in an experienced friend to help and advise every now and again for the first year. Horsemen and women are always willing to help the keen novice.

During winter months quite a lot of horses and ponies

46

Fig. 14. Trace clip suitable for pony

doing hard regular work are clipped. If our pony is kept at home and only ridden at week-ends, resist the temptation to have this done. He will look shaggy and rather untidy but he will be warm and comfortable so leave him the coat nature intended him to wear. Ponies doing regular hard work during the winter sweat profusely under their thick coats and this is clipped on to stop the excessive sweating which would otherwise result. A pony kept at a riding school in a stable and being ridden for an hour or two each day would, however, benefit from being fully clipped or trace-clipped. Trace clipping means leaving hair on the legs and a top 'blanket' of hair on the back and loins and having the head and neck clipped out.

The majority of ponies wear shoes on their feet for riding purposes. Brood mares, ponies kept for very small children and some native ponies may do without them but ponies to-day have an inevitable amount of roadwork and so in most cases shoeing is a necessity. You will be fortunate if there is a blacksmith in the immediate vicinity. They are now becoming more difficult to find because not very many young men are taking up the trade.

Most ponies are not taken to a blacksmith to have their shoes renewed until one drops off. They should in fact be taken for a regular inspection every two months or so. Most sets of shoes last about eight weeks, but, like children, some ponies wear their shoes down quicker than others. It will depend how much riding on tarmac the pony is given. A new set of shoes for a pony costs £2.

A loose shoe must be attended to immediately. If the shoe is wrenched off and lost, this is wasteful, as it may not be worn out and could be nailed on again. Also, loose shoes will render the pony liable to stumble and this is dangerous to the rider.

Grooming should be a regular chore but not, necessarily, a daily one. Particularly if the pony is kept out at grass. It takes time, and energy to do the job well so reserve it for week-ends.

Before you begin, tie the pony up. The pony's feet should first be picked out with the hoof pick. Start with the near-fore and the rear-hind before moving round to the off side. Run your hand down his shoulder, standing with your back to his head and he should be well used to the routine and will lift his foot obligingly. Work the hoof pick from heel to toe either side of the triangular horny centre part which is called the frog. The routine may be done both before and after exercise.

Mud may be brushed briskly off the legs with the dandy brush, provided that they are quite dry. Under the belly may be muddy as well but a wisp of straw is more practical for this area. To make a 'wisp', lay out some straw, sufficient to make a coil, fairly thick and about two feet long. Place your foot on one end and roll it tightly into a long twist. Tie a knot in the middle and bang it against the wall so that all loose ends fall from it. Damp it slightly and the 'wisp' is ready for use.

The pony may be brushed all over with the dandy brush

48

and then with the soft body-brush. Start at the top of the neck and work down the body with strong circular movements. Use the curry comb to clean the body-brush. Brush out mane and tail thoroughly with the dandy brush and then sponge eyes and nostrils with a damp sponge.

The mane and tail should not be tugged at indiscriminately with a comb. If you want the pony's tail 'pulled' so that it has a neat appearance at the top call in an expert to do it for you. But, remember once you start this that it will need regular 'pulling' so it is wiser to leave it as nature intended. Never cut your pony's mane with scissors. When brushing out the tail it is not sensible to stand directly behind the pony, but rather to one side and against his quarters.

Always make the pony presentable before going for a ride. Grooming is very enjoyable for the pony and for his owner. It is good exercise and tones up the pony's muscles and gives him a comfortable feeling of well-being.

The pony now being clean, it is time the beginner learnt the correct procedure for the maintenance of her tack. To-day, many riding schools and private owners resort to modern preparations like Flexalan, to keep their saddles and bridles soft and supple, in good condition, and, therefore safe. It is an excellent thing that these preparations have been evolved because it makes the riding master's task an easier one, and ensures that a lot of saddles and bridles are kept reasonably clean which would not otherwise be the case. The beginner, however, should be properly initiated in the best way to keep her tack clean and although this is an old-fashioned method which stud grooms and horse masters have been practising for years, it is still much the best and most efficient. A general rule in many establishments today seems to be to thoroughly clean all tack, in the manner to be described, once a week. This proves quite adequate unless the horses are being used for hunting or showing.

Cleaning utensils to be collected for the job are, a tin of saddle soap, a chamois leather, a soft polishing cloth (a discarded Harrington nappy is perfect), two sponges and a tin of metal polish. The saddle soap can be bought at any saddlers and at most hardware stores and will cost about 42½p. Some saddlers still stock bars of saddle soap and these are splendid to use, so buy one in preference to the tin, if you can find one.

Before starting work, assemble the above necessities and a bucket of warm water, in your harness room. This may be the stable, the garage or, I advise, the kitchen, in cold weather. But put plenty of newspapers down if you are going to work in there, because a certain amount of splashing and dripping will go on, and you may be unpopular.

Remove the curb chain from the bridle, if there is one and the stirrups from the stirrup leathers and put them in the bucket of water to soak. Take the whole bit off too if the reins and headpiece are buckled on and put it in to soak as well. If the leather pieces are stitched on this is, of course, impossible.

Loosen all buckles, and with one of the sponges dipped in the warm water, wash all the leather thoroughly, and the bit which may have dried saliva and grass adhering to it. Web or string girths should be brushed and if they are very dirty soak them in warm water with soap powder added and scrub them. Hang them on the pulley in the kitchen or put in the sun to dry.

When all the leather parts have been washed, dry them with the chamois leather and do not leave them to dry by themselves. This would soon render the leather hard and liable to crack.

Next, rub the other sponge dry on the saddle soap and commence soaping all the leather, this is the best part of tack cleaning and very satisfying work. Get into all the unseen parts like the inner flap of the saddle and the under flap of the stirrup leather guard and give special attention to all straps where they come into contact with a buckle. The reins must be kept soft and supple so sponge them well, they are easy to work with, and feel lovely when they are finished.

When the leather parts are finished, the bit and the stirrups may be dried with the soft cloth and then polished with metal polish.

Everything will now be clean, so the jigsaw puzzle of putting it all together again can begin. This is impossible to describe in writing but you will soon get used to where everything goes. After the first few muddles it is a fact that cleaning tack is a chore that when properly learnt is never forgotten. If your pony is kept at a riding school, someone there will be doing the job too, and will keep you right. Take a pride in the pony's belongings, and his appearance, and the work will be fun and immensely satisfying.

CHAPTER SEVEN

CATCHING, MOUNTING AND THE FIRST STEPS IN RIDING THE PONY

When the beginner's pony is housed at a riding school she will have the advantage of experts to help with the interesting business of saddling up and riding the new acquisition. Most riding schools are bewildering places for the novice. Much coming and going and chatter goes on, making this whole riding business seem a very jolly affair. This it will soon become for our beginner, as well, once she has mastered the rudiments of horse management. Nevertheless, try and remember when handling any pony that a noisy groom is not, necessarily, an efficient one. Some of the female staff at the riding centres seem to be under the mistaken illusion that the more bustle and noise they make, the better the impression they will give.

Horses prefer being handled by someone quiet and gentle, but firm and efficient. Some of the mounts at these establishments have probably become bored with routine and need hustling along, but our beginner's pony will not appreciate being dragged about. The practice of fine horsemanship begins before you arrive in the saddle and it is vital to cement the friendship, and trust, which will ultimately form between you both, whilst the various tasks are undertaken in preparation for mounting and going out riding together.

Keeping the new pony alone at home will mean that catching, saddling-up and embarking upon the first ride will be a much greater adventure. Try not to get worried and into a fluster at the first difficulties, because there will be some, and the owner's apprehension can be quickly communicated to her pony. If problems become overwhelming, call in a friend before you lose faith in yourself, anyone who keeps horses is always glad to help the novice. In a later

Fig. 15. Catching the pony

chapter I will tell you about the Pony Club, and Riding Clubs, and from these organisations, in your area, you will receive invaluable assistance. Riding for the beginner today is a lot easier than it was before the last war when only the privileged from riding families owned ponies, and the one-horse owner was very much on her own, with few authorities to turn to for help and encouragement.

Let us now presume that the new pony is in the paddock and the exciting moment has arrived when we shall catch him, saddle up, and set forth on our first ride together.

Catching the pony the right way is all-important. We must go about this confidently and lay the foundations of what we hope will be a lasting friendship.

Fetch the halter and walk towards the pony in the field taking with you a bowl of pony cubes. Call him up to you, 'Kup, Kup, Kup', he will soon learn to come to this. When you are nearly up to him, stand still and hold out the bowl. Let him sniff the cubes, he will love them, I have not yet met a horse or pony that didn't, and eat a few. When he is standing quietly and feeding, place the bowl on the grass and carefully slip your arm around his neck. Probably he will lift his head from munching and you can then easily slip on

53

Fig. 16. Correct way to lead pony

the halter. First, over the nose, and then pull the headpiece over the ears. This accomplished, and you can count yourself very fortunate. Your pony is one of those paragons who enjoy being caught and brought in to be ridden.

Should the pony seem nervous, however, and draw away when you slip your arm around his neck you must proceed with the utmost caution. Let him relax again and eat a few more mouthfuls. Do not make a grab at him but be patient. He will soon learn that he is not going to be hurt. Pick up the bowl before he finishes and walk back towards the gate and he will follow. Then feed him again, stroke him and he will let you slip your arm around his neck.

Lead him on the nearside, that is, on his left, and he walks on your right. This is the rule always, when leading a horse. Tie him up in the stable or to a ring outside the garage or wherever you have arranged to attend to his toilet.

Groom him now as described in the previous chapter and then fetch the saddle and bridle. The saddle is always put on first. Lay it carefully just behind the pony's withers, always sliding it back into the correct position rather than forward against the lie of the hair. Draw up the girth allowing room, when it is buckled up, for the tips of two fingers under the girth, but not any more. Adjust the stirrups to near the correct length by measuring them against your arm, with the right hand on the buckle and the left hand holding the stirrup iron which should reach your arm-pit. The exact length will only be decided when the rider is actually settled in the saddle.

Putting the bridle on is much more confusing for the novice and I do advise, if you have never attempted this before, to find a competent friend to help before you try it with a new pony. Actually, most ponies are quite co-operative about it all and mind much less than would be expected. After all, it cannot be comfortable to have the ears and mane tugged through the headpiece and a cold piece of ironmongery shoved between the teeth. No wonder some ponies do drop their heads at the vital moment or wander off as soon as the halter is slipped off to avoid the nuisance.

Get the assistant to stand on the other side of the pony's head to prevent any minor mishaps. Always put the reins round the pony's neck before slipping off the halter. By doing this, you do have some attachment to the animal when the halter is actually removed. With the right hand hold the bridle literally in front of his face, the bit hanging down below the pony's mouth. With the left hand put the bit in the pony's mouth, making him open his mouth by putting your thumb high up in his lips where he has no teeth. It is almost impossible to explain this to a complete novice so this is where, we hope, the assistant will be on hand to help. He will open his mouth to take the bit and, as he does so, simultaneously draw the headpiece over his forehead pushing his ears through as carefully as possible. Tidy the mane, arrange it carefully, and then draw up the throat lash allowing plenty of room between his throat and the strap. Fasten the nose band and the curb chain if he has one, which it is hoped he won't, as they are extremely awkward things for the beginner's fumbling fingers to put on straight.

At last the great moment has nearly arrived when our beginner can actually mount and settle herself in the saddle. Before doing this, button up your jacket, settle the hat firmly on the head, pull the stirrups down the leathers and draw the girth up another hole.

A good seat on a horse is the essence of good horsemanship and the aim of every novice who recognises how important this is. The idea is, to have a firm seat and light sensitive hands and, alas, how surprisingly difficult this is to achieve. Practically any horse will go kindly for those who do manage it. Nature never meant the horse to carry heavy weights on his back. So when a pony has saddle and bridle and child all upon his back, his head and neck and free natural movement are necessarily restricted. Thus, over the years, the correct seat has been adjusted to find the most comfortable position for rider and mount.

Study photographs of the experts in the saddle and ask the riding master at the school where you learnt to show you exactly how you ought to sit. This is better than a page of explanation. Good seats and good hands are not necessarily born in a rider but by concentration and determination they may be achieved by any rider who is the right build and who possesses the necessary balance.

There are various different ways of arriving in the saddle but they only differ in minor forms. The important thing to bear in mind is not to poke your toe too sharply into the pony's stomach, nor to land with too heavy a thud on his back. If the rider does this, the pony will soon take a dislike to being mounted and will move off whenever he is mounted and this becomes a very tiresome habit.

Stand on the pony's nearside, with your left shoulder close to his shoulder and yourself facing his tail. Grasp the reins in the left hand and hold them just by the pony's withers. With the right hand, take hold of the stirrup and place your left foot in it. Then grasp hold of the back of the saddle with

Fig. 17. Correct position of rein in hand. 1. Riding. 2. Driving

the right hand and hoist yourself up with a light spring. Swing the right leg across the pony's back and let yourself gently down into the saddle.

This is not as confusing as it may sound. Try it first with an assistant holding the pony's head, then you can relax and will not be worried about whether he is going to walk off at the crucial moment. After the first half dozen times, mounting will become a perfectly simple manoeuvre and it needs very little skill to do it well. If the pony is rather tall, take him alongside a mounting block or a gate whilst learning. Scrambling breathlessly up on to a high mount is an unpromising way to begin a ride and, anyway, it is undignified and uncomfortable.

The rider having successfully achieved the saddle, she should try and relax for a few minutes and settle herself into a comfortable position. No daylight should be seen between the knees and the saddle and the legs from thigh to calf should be pressed against the pony's sides. The ball of the foot rests on the stirrup iron and the toe inclines upwards. Sit well down in the saddle with the back straight, but not rigid and with the head up and yourself looking between the pony's ears.

The reins are held now in both hands, the fingers bent and thumbs uppermost with the rein coming between the third and little finger and again between thumb and forefinger. Get the riding master to show you several times how to do this and sit and practise it so that it comes naturally. A very good idea is to imagine that you have the bit in your own mouth and then you can much better appreciate what it feels like to be guided by reins. The idea is to maintain a

57

light firm contact, the reins being regarded as contact lines and not ropes to hang on by.

Before urging our mount forward it would really be wise to learn how to dismount from the saddle. This is an even simpler process than getting into it. At a riding establishment this will not normally be taught until the end of the lesson, but the beginner rider who is going to be alone quite soon must learn all these elementary movements as quickly as possible.

In order to get both feet on the ground again, put both reins in the left hand and kick both feet free of the stirrups. Place the right hand on the pommel, or front arch of the saddle and throwing the right leg over the back of the saddle, slide carefully to the ground. Always take both feet out of the stirrups before dismounting. It seems a common mistake for beginners to leave the left foot in its iron and this could be dangerous if the pony moved off in the middle, causing his rider to hop precariously after him whilst trying to disengage the left foot.

After this rather unpleasant thought we had better return to the saddle, and the exciting moment when the novice and his new pony are going to leave the yard and embark upon their first real ride together.

CHAPTER EIGHT

ELEMENTARY SCHOOLING AND USE OF THE AIDS. GATES, AND WHAT TO DO WHEN OUT FOR A RIDE

The rider gives her pony signals by the use of hands, legs and voice to indicate to him what she wishes he should do next. These signals are known as the aids. Artificial aids are whips, spurs and complicated bits, but the beginner must, at all costs, avoid adopting these measures which should be handled by experienced riders to be at all effective.

Many ponies, upon which the novice rider must learn, are unresponsive to the natural aids. This is because they have been ridden by beginners who are constantly misapplying the signals so that the ponies learn to be long-suffering and patient and soon do not hurry to respond. Many riding school ponies become, in time, immune to anything less than a hearty kick. Nevertheless, the novice should learn the correct way to apply the aids to the schooled, responsive pony, so that she knows what she is aiming at. Also, she might be lucky enough to find she has bought a well-schooled pony who will respond correctly.

We now wish to leave the proximity of the stable, so the beginner must apply the correct aid to stir her pony from halt to walk. Apply pressure with legs and heels just behind the girth, at the same time relaxing the feel on the reins. The ideal, actually, is not to have to kick, but simply to squeeze, in order that he should respond. Watch those beautifully schooled hacks in the show ring. Their riders do not have to flap their legs to achieve results. But it is quite possible that nothing short of a kick will shift our beginner's mount so do not hesitate to do this, if it proves necessary.

When he is walking forward, try and sit still, relaxed and as comfortable as possible, guiding him into the paddock or down a convenient lane. His own field is not, actually, an

Fig. 18. The right way to apply the 'aids' – the wrong way

ideal place in which to do elementary schooling. He will have his favourite corner, and tree, and will probably think it a good idea to make tracks for them or for the gate and his mind will not be on the job.

Keep the pony going nicely at the walk until you have got the feel of him, and keep him going at a steady pace by using pressure with the legs against his sides. He may attempt to graze or snatch at tasty branches but make it quite clear to him that you will stand no nonsense and these temptations must be resisted.

The beginner will find the trot quite the worst part about learning to ride. Every novice takes time to master this pace and finds it most uncomfortable while doing so. Before she has a pony of her own she must get this elementary part of riding conquered during those early lessons at the riding school. Bumping about alone on a new pony will not do. So resolve to master this pace before the pony is bought. After several lessons the rhythm of the step will come. Try to rise from the knees rather than the stirrups and do not rise too high out of the saddle. A regular rhythmic movement will soon become automatic and then it is not at all uncomfortable.

Trot slowly, going too fast will throw the beginner about in the saddle too much. Try and keep a feel on the pony's mouth during these paces without holding him too short, or letting the reins hang too loose. So easy to write, but it is not easy to achieve this ideal contact. The exact pressure will come by experience, as the rider learns how responsive to the feel of the reins her pony is.

Schooling the pony in circles is valuable practice and may be done, first at the walk and then at a trot. This will help the pony to relax and to become more obedient. Bending in and out of straw bales lying in stubble fields is great fun and very good practice. Well-schooled ponies can make quite small neat circles, but a stiff or unbalanced pony finds this very difficult. Teach him to circle correctly by leaning to the right or to the left as he comes round, and try hard not to haul him round. Work at a slow pace rather than a fast one as this will help to keep him correctly balanced.

The transition from trot to canter is a delightful one. Once the beginner has mastered the trot and can allow her pony to break into a canter she will discover, with joy, just what riding is all about. This is a comfortable, even, stride, and when the rider can learn to sit down in the saddle and go with her pony she will be well on the way to becoming a good rider. You will see people who stand up in their stirrups at the canter or roll about hilariously with hands high and legs loosely flapping. This is not the way to ride a fast pace.

The gallop can be quite alarming for a novice because most horses and ponies go into this pace from a canter and become quite unbalanced and excited, and give the unfortunate novice an uncomfortable feeling of being out of control – which, indeed, she probably will be.

As the pace quickens, and the pony goes faster, his body becomes lower, and he must stretch his neck out. The rider leans slightly forward and shortens her reins. As riding experience progresses, and the urge to go faster comes, then the novice should look for a gentle uphill stretch of grass where the pony will break into a canter without becoming uncontrolled and where the rider will easily be able to pull up.

Having learnt about the different paces at which she is going to proceed, when out for a ride, it is all-important that our beginner knows the correct way to stop. This does not mean a drag on the reins or several hearty hauls on the pony's mouth. Some ponies may have developed hard mouths, particularly from long use in riding schools, and will require a pull on the mouth, but the correct aid to achieve a smooth transition from walk to halt is, as follows : Close the legs, that is, press with the inside of both legs, and, at the same time, increase the tension on the reins by a gentle pull. Say 'whoa' in a long drawn-out tone, he will probably be used to this. When the pony stops, he should be standing squarely on all four legs, with head held up and not dragged into his chest by the rider's heavy contact with the reins. By using legs as well as reins to halt, the pony will remain balanced and collected.

When our beginner is out for a ride on her new pony we assume that she is going to have to encourage him, by the use of the above aids, to quicken his pace. If, however, he does not heed this encouragement and sets the pace himself, then the rider has made a mistake and must quickly rectify it before too late. No beginner should learn on a pony which goes too fast for her. It is alarming, and can be very frightening, to have the feeling that she might not be able to stop when she has not yet even mastered the correct method of how to do so. The pony must go back from whence he came before our novice rider's nerve is broken.

This is why ponies go out on trial, so that would-be purchasers may discover how keen a pony is. When a trial is not allowed, expert friends must advise and try the pony. No beginner would be allowed a pony which is too keen. Much better have a lazy one. Bad habits, such as kicking and flapping of reins may develop, but these faults can be later eradicated as confidence grows and the pony improves. Lost confidence takes a terrible lot of retrieving and can so easily be gone for ever.

After the pupil has been riding her pony satisfactorily for a while and progress with the aids is becoming more natural, the rider will benefit her natural seat by, either, riding without stirrups or without the saddle at all. Many children, who own their own ponies, become quite adept at riding bareback. Ten minutes a day is adequate to start with, as it does impose a strain on slack muscles, but trotting and cantering about with no stirrups helps to develop a strong seat and good balance.

Where to ride in many areas, today, is becoming a serious problem. This is why it is most important to look carefully into the question of private ownership before the pony is purchased and the undoubtedly very useful, riding school abandoned.

It is not possible for the rider to gallop happily about neighbouring fields without the permission of the farmer who owns the land. Parents of children and young people who own ponies must become aware of this. Farming is becoming progressively more intensive and every acre now has to earn its keep. Children living in suburban areas may have a serious problem about where to ride and these are the riders who would do much better to stick to riding at an establishment.

If you do want to ride near home and there is scope for this, go and visit the farmers and ask permission before trespassing. Some of them will be sympathetic and will give it. Never ride over growing crops and seeds and always shut gates to avoid stock straying. If the chain was on the gate when you rode up to it, that chain must be replaced on its keeper when you leave it. Never ride in a field where you see a loose horse grazing. The loose animal will gallop about upsetting the rider's mount and it will not be easy to get out of the field without the loose horse getting out too. So avoid this situation at all costs.

Enquire if the riding school where you learnt to ride belongs to an organisation called a 'Rider's Association'. It may have a variation in name in the area, but these groups are being formed now with the object of investigating the problem of where to ride. In Surrey, for example, a problem has arisen due to the amount of common land in the county, upon which control is difficult, and too many riders are spoiling the turf, and the amenities, for the hundreds of pedestrians who also like to enjoy the commons. Riding schools, riding clubs, and pony clubs, wish to co-operate with local authorities, in this, and similar problems existing in other areas. Find out what the situation is in your part of the country, before buying a pony.

Riding on the highways today is a very hazardous undertaking. Do not venture on to main roads at all until you have been riding a long time and you know your mount is foolproof where cars and lorries are concerned. Even the quietest pony can shy when a long distance lorry driver releases his vehicle's airbrakes with a shriek as it slows down, which they do not all do. Some very nasty accidents have occurred on main roads in recent years. The danger to horses and horsemen cannot be stressed too highly, so beginners must, at all costs, keep off tarmac.

When experience has been gained and the need to ride on the road does arise, study the section of the Highway Code first which refers to riders. Always acknowledge the courtesy of drivers who slow down. This will help to encourage motorists to extend this courtesy to other riders, it is a pity so few do.

It is fun to ride in company and the novice will enjoy herself more, and will learn more quickly, if she can find a companion in the area to ride with. Join the local riding club, or pony club branch, and riding friends will soon materialise. The beginner's pony will go much better for her with some company. Be careful to keep a length away from the other ponies' heels and dissuade friends from racing about as this will upset our beginner's pony. Anyway, it is not necessary to gallop hilariously about to enjoy yourself out riding.

When a companion opens a gate out riding, always wait until he has shut it again before riding on yourself. Opening gates is an important part of riding which we must learn before we can go for a proper ride.

Fig. 19. Practise opening gates

The correct procedure, on approaching a gate, is to take both reins in the right hand and to ride up alongside the gate so that it is possible to reach down and undo the latch with the left hand. The rider then reins back, drawing the gate open. Prop the gate ajar and ride through slowly. Do not allow the pony to scramble hurriedly through. He may catch his hip bone, or your knee, which will be most painful, and he must learn to be patient, because there will often be occasions when the gate will need holding open for companions, either on rides together, or out hunting. When the rider has come through she must then turn the pony back and make him stand quietly while she fastens the catch. When the catch is on the other end of the gate to the above description, then take both reins in the left hand and open the gate with the right.

Riding up and downhill is very good training for pony and rider. Walking and slow trotting up slopes will help to get the animal fit quicker than any amount of fast work. Riding up hill, lean forward and try to 'go with' your mount, leaving him a loose rein so that he can stretch out his neck. Grasp the mane, if necessary, to prevent the sensation of being 'left behind'. Coming down hill, grip with the knees, try to keep the legs straight and don't allow the pony to turn sideways, especially on a steep slope. Thus, if he slips going straight, he will only slide on to his haunches.

Do not arrive back in the stable yard at a fast pace. If the pony gets accustomed to coming in at a spanking trot he will begin prancing each time you near home because he anticipates home comforts and the hurry to get there. If he is sweating, he must be rubbed down with a wisp, particularly in the girth and saddle area, and behind the ears, before being turned out to graze.

CHAPTER NINE

MORE ADVANCED SCHOOLING FOR PONY AND RIDER. ELEMENTARY JUMPING

Elementary riding, and schooling, will gradually lead to more advanced work. Pony and rider will become more ambitious as mutual confidence grows. Hacking about the countryside will help to achieve this and the walk, trot, canter and simple aids will soon be mastered. More advanced work, however, will have to be done in the school and this is where the excellent riding schools and equitation centres are doing such splendid work today. The whole standard of riding has gone up and the immense value of school work, where riders can be properly trained, has now been appreciated and is being exploited to the full.

A school, in riding language, is a level space, indoors or outdoors, where horses and riders are trained. It may be a large building with a soft, peat floor, or an outdoor school which has been fenced, and given a top coat of cinders, or it may be the corner of a field which an enthusiast has marked out with oil drums, stones or posts. Anyone who marks one out for herself should make the school area not less than twenty-two yards by forty-four, the school thus being oblong in shape.

Ten minutes work in the school every morning before setting out for a ride will be valuable. The work can be varied, and the various paces practised, and in this way, more will be achieved than might be, during the course of the ride. Teach the pony to walk out well and to keep his head up and himself alert. If he is a very slow walker, try giving him a sharp tap with your stick, rather than constant kicking, which is tiring for the rider. Change direction now and then and work diagonally across the school to do this. As the rider becomes more experienced, try and do some schooling at the sitting trot, notice the experts doing this at equitation centres and in the show ring. You will see them doing this riding around corners. Also, as their mount strikes off into a canter, and to enable the animal to lengthen his stride at the trot and extend himself as he passes the judges.

Learning the sitting trot is not as difficult as it may at first feel, and it certainly does feel very uncomfortable to start with. Practise with feet in the stirrups, sitting deeply in the saddle with feet and legs in the right place and body upright, but not stiffly erect. Gripping with the knees should be avoided as this will have the effect of making the rider sit on top of the saddle, rather than in it, and the object of the sitting trot will be lost. It is surprising how quickly the rhythm does come.

Some exercises in the saddle, whilst the pony is stationary in the centre of the school, are a good plan for novice riders. They help to develop a strong seat and a firm grip. Get an assistant to stand and hold the pony's head whilst you do these exercises. No one experienced will be necessary, a brother or sister would be quite adequate for this job. They will just have to stop the pony wandering off whilst you are busy touching your toes, or dropping his head to crop the grass at the wrong moment.

A good exercise is to drop the reins and lean right back until the back of the head rests on the pony's quarters, the rider's legs, meanwhile, being kept in the correct position against the pony's sides. With hands on hips the rider then must try to rise again slowly from the waist. An assistant at the pony's head is very necessary during this exercise.

Another exercise is to lean down and touch each toe alternately over the pony's withers with the opposite hand. Whilst doing this exercise, the object is to try to keep the seat well down in the saddle and the legs in the correct position. Regain a good seat in the saddle by bracing yourself from the waist and not by supporting yourself with the hands.

'Going round the world' is an exercise which most children enjoy. An assistant must again be at the pony's head whilst this one is accomplished. Drop the reins and throw one leg over the pony's withers so that you are sitting sideways in the saddle. Then, the opposite leg goes over the pony's quarters so that you are facing the pony's tail and so you go round until the correct position is regained. Nervous riders may not like this one, but it is a very suppling exercise and fun to perform.

Exercises may be done without the saddle too and some riders find them easier to perform like this.

Reining back, is one of the first steps in school work that pony and rider will have to master. Try it first dismounted. Stand in front of the pony, holding a rein in each hand a few inches from the bit ring on each side of his mouth. Press on the reins and say 'back', he will arch his neck and mouth the bit, but in due course, he will obey. Tread gently on the coronet of the hoof, if he is slow to respond, or let go one rein and tap his knee with your stick, don't jab him in the mouth and raise your voice in exasperation. As he responds and steps back a pace or two, relax pressure on the rein and praise him. Running back is quite wrong, he must learn to go back sedately and controlled. When he becomes quite good at this, try it mounted, giving a pull on the reins and giving the command and slackening the reins immediately he obeys. The value of having mastered this exercise will be fully appreciated when you graduate to the show ring and the hunting field.

Try not to get careless and think that this school work is a waste of time. These exercises are tremendously important and will lay the foundations of understanding between pony and rider better than hours of riding about the countryside will do. It may take six months before the pony responds, and real progress is made, but it will be well worth it in the end. Ten minutes each morning before your ride will be quite enough in the school. Too long will bore the pony, anyway, and his attention will wander and he will not respond when he becomes bored.

Before closing this chapter about learning to ride, and

progressing to more ambitious things, a short description of elementary jumping will be valuable. Every new rider looks at the jumps and longs to be having a try 'over the sticks'. She is sure to attempt to do this before she and her pony are ready, most beginners do. So it might be as well to learn the right way to go about it.

The best way to begin jumping is to encounter small obstacles during the course of the morning's ride. Ditches, logs and branches make splendid first jumps. The pony will take them in his stride and they will be negotiated with little effort. When a small jump looms ahead, try not to clutch the reins and crouch over the withers – the natural position for every beginner when an obstacle is first encountered. Neither will it do to let him slow down to a walk as he realises what is expected of him, and then to give him a kick in the ribs and a shout of command and allow him to leap over from a standstill. Most unseating and uncomfortable for the rider, and the pony will receive a jab in the mouth, which will not encourage him to try again another time.

As the pony approaches a small suitable obstacle, shorten the reins just a little, keep the hands low on the withers, keep the heels down and press the calves against his sides to keep him going. If he should show signs of hesitating, try to keep calm, urge him on with the legs and voice and he will hop over quite easily.

Get used to small obstacles out riding, scramble up and down banks and over ditches, and confidence will grow and, daily, it will all become more fun and less alarming. Then build some small jumps in the school ring at home. Or, perhaps jumping lessons are being taken at the riding school. A course of half-a-dozen lessons for our beginner, and her pony, under an expert would be invaluable, so try and arrange this, before continuing with more advanced work at home.

When building some jumps at home, arrange the obstacles in a circle, rather than a straight line, because this excites a pony less than when he is faced with a line of

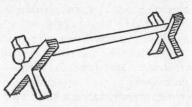

Fig. 20. Cavalletti

fences. The jumps need not, in fact, should not, be elaborate, but make them strong and not liable to collapse or he
will quickly become careless.

Fathers and brothers make useful aides when jumps have
to be constructed. A small wall, a brush fence and a pole
jump would be splendid. Construct wings to the obstacles
so that you can concentrate upon how to sit and follow
through with the pony, without having to worry about him
running out on the approach.

If it is possible to spend some money on some jumps, do
not be tempted into elaborate coloured gates and expensive
artificial walls. What our beginner needs are a collection of
obstacles called 'cavalletti'. Every riding establishment in the
country, of any merit at all, will possess some. These can be
adequately constructed at home by nailing short pieces of
wood together to form a cross, and then fixing a strong and
solid looking pole between two of them. The value of this
simple obstacle, is that, it may be put at three different
heights depending upon the way it is laid on the ground.
Four cavalletti would be splendid for this preliminary
training.

Keep the jumps quite low until you feel comfortable getting over them, then you can raise them slightly and the
difference in the movement should be slight with no discomfort to yourself or your pony.

Ten minutes schooling over your jumps, each morning,
will be enough. Do not sicken the pony or he may become
bored and careless as a result. This will mean unnecessary

refusing and running out. A friend, with a pony who is a reliable jumper, would be most helpful, so try and persuade her to come and give you a lead over your small fences. This will hearten your mount, he will enjoy the company and it is fun to ride follow-my-leader over the jumps.

It is not policy here to start explaining what our pupil should do if her new pony does not know how to jump, or, worse still, knows only too well, and begins prancing and sweating at sight of an obstacle. Beginners should not be teaching beginners, harm will be done to one or the other, or both. The novice's pony must know how to jump, and be willing to do it kindly, before they can make a good job of the work together.

Top: The Fell pony, an ideal type used for pony trekking

Centre: Pupils at a school of equitation where instruction of a fairly advanced nature is given. Note the alert expression of the horses and their well-kept appearance. Riding clothes are more orthodox on a holiday of this nature

Left: More people than ever before are interested in what their local pack of hounds has to offer

Cross country events provide a very interesting selection of obstacles

Another interesting obstacle typical of the cross-country phase

Show jumping has caught the imagination of millions of horse lovers all over the world

A pony can provide fun and enjoyment for children in a variety of ways

At many centres each guest is
allotted to a pony for the
duration of the holiday and will
gain much satisfaction and
pleasure from the association

Bringing the ponies in from the field is the start of the day's work

Top: Mounting and adjusting the stirrups to the correct length. These ponies are at a trekking establishment which explains the headcollars and ropes under the bridles and the raincoats rolled up in front of the saddles. *Centre:* Instruction will be given in most establishments when clients wish it. As will be seen from the photographs, some visitors are already experienced and others need help in the elements of horsemastership. Note the wide range of garments which are worn on many riding holidays. *Bottom:* The leader of the party is taking his group for a turn around the stable yard to allow them to get the feel of the saddle and to become accustomed to handling their ponies before embarking upon a ride in the open country

Saddled and bridled and ready for the ride. Many establishments use covered yards like this where there is a shortage of stabling

Drawing up the girths before going out to mount

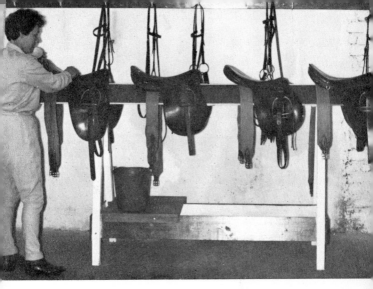

Keeping the tack clean is very important. Note the clean and tidy appearance of this saddle room

Fox hunting is a wonderful sport for the rider and appeals to young and old

Out for a ride. These ponies are following too closely to one another. Ideally they should be a pony's length apart or be riding abreast. The first rider is the only one correctly turned out with a hard riding hat

This photograph serves to illustrate how the riding party conducts itself along a road. Where only one operator goes out with the party she generally prefers to ride out in front and to put a reasonably experienced rider to bring up the rear. Note the typically pleasant riding

CHAPTER TEN

SOME PONY PROBLEMS

Problems with ponies do arise, alas, however much we would like to do without them. Even the nicest pony, suitable for a beginner, can develop the odd trick or habit, which may, unless it is understood, and checked correctly, develop into serious misbehaviour. Very often, the rider, herself, may have allowed the trouble to develop, simply through ignorance of the right way to deal with it.

A happy partnership should exist between pony and rider, a mutual understanding born of confidence in one another and enjoyment in what can be achieved together. But, one of the pair must have the upper hand, and there should be no doubt, whatever, which of the two this will be. The rider will act as guide and mentor, and her pony will do as he is told, confidently and eagerly, we hope. Should the pony develop into the boss, disaster will lie ahead for the beginner. Do not hesitate to call in expert help, at once, if there are signs of this happening.

Ponies must be ridden and handled regularly if they are to remain obedient, and this must be borne in mind when the pony is bought. A common cause of misbehaviour is overfeeding and under-exercising. Here again we find the benefit of keeping the novice's pony in an establishment where he can be regularly worked. Dark evenings, and the pressure of school work, do not allow of much opportunity for evening riding.

A pony that is under-exercised and overfed, may develop a tendency to shy. This means that he swings round or leaps into the air in a most disconcerting, and unseating, fashion, whenever he is asked to pass anything that he considers alarming or unusual. He will begin pretending to see bogies in hedges and to hear monsters snorting under the bonnets of innocent stationary cars. As he was not in the habit of indulging in such fancies when he was bought as a quiet, beginner's pony, he is merely bored and fresh and this naughtiness must be checked.

The main thing to remember, when a pony starts to shy unnecessarily, is that his rider must remain confident, and firm, and not begin clutching the reins apprehensively. Otherwise, her nervousness will quickly communicate itself to her mount with results which may be imagined. He will think it is great fun to frighten his rider and this he will not hesitate to try and do, henceforth, at every opportunity.

As soon as the pony shies, or shows any inclination to stop and snort unnecessarily at various objects he must be turned firmly round and ridden up to the offending object. He must be made to drop his head and sniff it, and keep on looking at it, until he is thoroughly bored and repentant. So he will understand, quite clearly, that his rider is not amused by his capers and has no intention of allowing him to get away with such a silly habit.

Young ponies, which shy at traffic and alarming obstructions, must be treated with care and respect, or they may be genuinely frightened, but this training of novice ponies must not come within the scope of this book.

A pony may buck out of high spirits and a feeling of wellbeing and when the rider knows her pony, and has confidence in him, then a few small bucks will not worry her at all. In fact, she may enjoy them, if they are not persistent and too unseating, they are a means of the pony's need to show his exuberance. But a hearty buck, when the pony drops his head and arches his back, is not pleasant and steps must be taken at once to correct this habit before it develops further.

Riding along, a pony will nearly always give himself away if he is thinking of indulging in a buck. The most likely place for him to do it will be the first nice big green field that you enter. Ponies do not buck on roads, which is fortunate, as they would be horribly hard to fall on. He will probably lay his ears back and try to drop his head and he may even give a squeal of devilment before he puts his head between his knees and kicks up his heels. The rider must shorten the reins and take a firm hold on his head, to keep it up, when she senses that he is about to buck and must drive the pony on with pressure of knees and calves and, if necessary, the voice. He cannot possibly buck if his head is up. Ponies may buck, of course, because they are uncomfortable but would generally do so, in this case, before leaving the stable yard. Check that girths are not twisted or drawn up too tightly.

A pony which rears, has an unpleasant habit of standing up on his hind legs without any warning and sometimes in the most awkward situations. As it is possible that he could come over backwards when he does this, it is a very salutary and unpleasant experience and any pony with the slightest tendency to rear must not be ridden by a novice.

Another annoying habit is kicking and generally ponies do this out of fear or nervousness and not from naughtiness. Though not as disastrous as rearing it is, nevertheless, tiresome, and the rider must not give him the opportunity to do it. She will not suffer from the habit, but her friends and their ponies will. Take the hind shoes off, and tie a small red bow on his tail, and do not ride through crowded gateways out hunting or put him in the position where he might hurt someone.

A puller is a very exhausting ride and the quickest way to give a beginner bad hands is to put her on a pony with a hard mouth. Your pony, when it arrived, will not have been a puller but this tendency can develop, especially when you progress to going out hunting together. Ponies start to pull because they are keen and excited and it is advisable not to immediately put him in a double bridle or a drop noseband. These remedies do not cure and may render his mouth more insensible.

Concentrate on some schooling, trying to get the pony nicely balanced, and, using a snaffle bit, try to make him obedient and improve his mouth. Ride in circles and give him plenty of reining back work. Never gallop him about with other ponies or give him oats.

These days of mechanised transport will probably mean that your pony will have to travel in a horse-box at some time or another. It is very important, therefore, that he approves of this mode of transport and will enter a vehicle without fuss or bother. Nothing is more exasperating than being offered a lift home from hunting, when you are a matter of ten miles from home, and your animal flatly refuses to climb the ramp to avail himself of the ride. With a young pony, or one which has had little experience of horse-boxes, much can be done to overcome his reluctance. A little patience and time spent on some lessons and he will soon learn.

It will be necessary to find a friend who will allow you to use his wagon trailer or horse-box for a few days. You could ride over to his yard and practise there. Lead the pony to the ramp and let him sniff it and realise that there is nothing to be afraid about. Be sure that the ramp is not placed at too steep an angle. No self-respecting pony is going to climb up a perpendicular ramp which clatters and sways when he puts his weight on it. Do not stand half way up and tug on the reins but show him a bowl of pony cubes and let him understand that he will have them as soon as he chooses to enter the box. Be patient and let him go on standing there until he is bored and appreciates that there really is nothing to fear. If you can arrange for a pony companion to be put in the box before him this will be an incentive and should greatly help to overcome his reluctance.

When he climbs the ramp and stands inside eating his reward, make much of him and tell him how obliging he has been, although it may have taken several days to achieve this end result. Repeat the lesson for several more days until he climbs in quite willingly and enjoys his feed in a calm relaxed fashion, when he gets there.

It is not unusual to find a pony which dislikes being ridden

76

through water. Why this should be so, it is difficult to understand, because, apart from being cold and wet, fording a stream is a harmless thing to ask a pony to do. But if he is obstinate about water it is really quite impossible to drag him through it, the same as it would be to drag him up a ramp into a horse-box. With the water problem we are at a disadvantage, because riders do not generally carry bowls of pony cubes about with them on rides, and neither do they care to stand in the middle of a ford trying to persuade their mounts to follow them through it.

Regular visits will have to be made to the ford of a river or a small stream in the immediate neighbourhood. Take a mounted friend with you, if possible. Kick some water up on to the pony's legs, so that he sees there is nothing to fear, and produce some cubes from your pocket to encourage him. His unwillingness will disappear as he grows confident and when he enters the water he will quite possibly go to the opposite extreme and start pawing the water with forefoot with the intention, next, of lying down and having a roll! It is remarkable how many ponies with an aversion to water also seem to have a tendency to lie down in it. It is a not uncommon sight, out hunting, when fording a stream to see some unfortunate child having to jump off her pony as he prepares to go down on his knees.

It would be very helpful to arrange to ride through a ford on the way home from exercising as often as possible. Looking forward to a return to home and supper, the pony will soon overcome his reluctance. Urge him on with voice and legs once he goes into the water to give him no opportunity to start splashing about. If he does start, a smart rap on the quarters with the riding cane will do the trick.

A nappy pony, is one which is spiteful and cross, in stable. Although we hope that our beginner's pony will not have a temperament like this, there are degrees of nappiness and a pony which is a delightful ride and cross in the stable might still be considered suitable for a sensible novice. Practically every pony like this, has become so through rough handling during young impressionable years, and he should be greatly improved by patient, gentle handling. Even vicious horses can be made tractable by patience and so there is hope for every small pony which has a tendency to be bad-tempered during grooming or saddling up. Quite possibly the girths may have been roughly drawn up and the skin pinched, when he was quite young, or he may have been poked sharply by a hay-fork or broom by a careless groom.

Confidence will be restored by the new owner of the pony taking pains always to be quiet and gentle in the stable and spending as much time with him as possible so that he will realise that he is not going to be hurt. Should the pony have a habit of nipping, he should be scolded immediately he does this. Obviously, a really vicious pony is not going to be cured by a novice, and there will be no pleasure for either, so it is not suggested that this sort of animal will do at all. Only, it is well to remember, that minor degrees of nappiness are not insurmountable difficulties and can quite definitely be completely eradicated.

Although the following small problem cannot be regarded as a vice, it is very common, and extremely tiresome, and any rider could cure the pony of the habit. Some ponies are very annoying about the business of being mounted and as soon as they feel the rider's foot in the stirrup, away they wander, leaving the unfortunate rider hopping after them. Most irritating and uncomfortable, but quite easily cured with patience.

Any pony, who has developed this habit, has either been carelessly mounted in the past, or has not been schooled properly to stand during his early training. Probably, his previous owner gave him a hearty tug in the mouth whilst she negotiated an ungainly scramble into the saddle, landing with a heavy bump. No wonder he learnt to dislike the process and chose to walk away to rid himself of the nuisance.

If there is a mounting block in the yard, then use it. It makes the job much easier especially when the rider is not very agile. Get an assistant to stand at the pony's head, in front of him, not to the side, and as soon as the rider prepares to mount, the assistant can restrain the pony from moving off. A few pony cubes should be given to reward him for standing quite still. Repeat this each time the pony is mounted for a week. By the end of that time he will have got the message and be much more interested in receiving his titbit than in walking away. The rider, meanwhile, must take pains to mount carefully without pulling the pony's mouth and dragging the saddle half off his back.

The next step is for the assistant to stand beside, rather than in front of, the pony's head. Thus, the pony learns to turn his head to receive his reward. In a few days, the rider can dispense with her assistance and lean down to reward the pony herself from her own pocket. He will look for this and will turn his head expectantly as soon as the weight is in the saddle. Always mount carefully after this and avoid scrambling on carelessly so that he does not get impatient again.

Solving a small problem, like this, together, will help to cement the friendship and will give a worthwhile sense of achievement.

Another minor difficulty may be the pony who does not care to have his bridle put on. He will probably hold his head up so high that it is impossible to get the hand up to pull the ears through the headpiece. Get a box or stool and place it on the pony's near side, turning him away from the manger and into one corner alongside the wall. Thus, he cannot swing away and the rider can pat him, and speak to him, and put the bridle on carefully, being sure she does not drag his ears or pull his mane roughly. As his confidence is restored, so the job will become easier and the pedestal put away. Should this habit persist, and he is not responding satisfactorily, call in an experienced friend to help and advise, before it gets any worse.

Ponies which are bad to catch are a terrible bore. Volumes of words have been written in horsemastership books, describing how best to tackle this very real problem. Suffice it to say, here, that a pony which refuses to be caught is not the slightest use to a novice. She cannot know how to cope with the coaxing and the tempting and wiles and schemes which must be thought up to get hold of the pony in an unguarded moment. It is extremely tiresome to set aside an hour for riding and then to have to spend three-quarters of it persuading the pony to be caught.

There are, of course, like other bad habits, degrees of this, and if the pony is quite young, the trouble will probably be quickly overcome by an experienced person, who will turn the pony out with a headcollar on and proceed with extreme caution to overcome his reluctance to be handled.

But this is no job for a beginner. Ponies with this problem should be avoided at all costs, or most of the joy of ownership will be lost.

There really are very few inherently wicked ponies about, and a novice owner would be most unlikely to find herself in possession of one, if she has taken pains to go about buying her pony in the manner described in earlier chapters of this book. Any of these difficulties, if they do not respond to the orthodox methods mentioned, would certainly respond to help from an experienced horseman, so never hesitate to call on sympathetic help. Carrying on blindly, and miserably, doing the wrong thing the wrong way and wondering why results are unsatisfactory, is merely foolish. The partnership must be a happy one, with mutual understanding, and no distrust, between pony and rider, or progress will never be made.

CHAPTER ELEVEN

THE PONY CLUB AND WHAT IT HAS TO OFFER THE BEGINNER TO RIDING. RIDING CLUBS

Now that we have learnt how to ride, and are reasonably competent, it is time to look about, and to find companions to ride with and ways and means to improve and to enjoy this wonderful new hobby.

Those who ride today are, indeed, very fortunate. The British Horse Society, about which, more will be told in a later chapter, have two wonderful organisations affiliated to them, and both of them are eminently suitable for beginners.

The oldest, and best-known of these two schemes, is the Pony Club, and the help and encouragement that this organisation has given to its members is beyond all praise. The movement started in 1928 with quite humble beginnings and in 1970, membership has reached 31,728, with some 287 branches in Great Britain. Each branch is administered by a District Commissioner, and a local committee, and members may belong to the Club until they are 21 years of age.

The growth of the Pony Club in its early years was gradual and it is interesting to consider its development. The first branch to be formed was the Old Surrey, now the Old Surrey and Burstow and then the North and South Shropshire, which have since divided. Thirdly, the Grafton, of which branch one of the first three members was the well-known personality who we all know from T.V. equine broadcasts today, Mr Dorian Williams.

In 1931, Colonel the Hon. Guy Cubitt, M.F.H., became interested in the Pony Club, and from its infancy, he has brought the club to the impressive position that it holds today. No one connected with the Pony Club has given more in time and effort than Colonel Cubitt. He was elected chairman of the club in 1947, when the, then, Institute of the Horse and Pony Club, and the National Horse Association, amalgamated, and became the British Horse Society.

The original idea was, that each Hunt should form a branch in its area and when there was no Hunt, the branch was called by the name of the town or locality. This idea, basically, still holds good, although to a certain extent, the character of the movement has undergone some change since its inception. The majority of members used to be farmers' children, and children of Hunt members, who all, or nearly all, owned their own ponies. Studying membership of the different branches, today, the position has altered considerably. A large number of members have no ponies of their own, but patronise local riding schools in their areas, and hire ponies for the various fixtures held by their own branch. Many members seem to be without much equine help or background in the home, so that their need for active assistance and service is pressing.

Membership subscription, in 1970, stood at £1 per annum, with an entrance fee of 12½p. Surely, the best value for money any young rider could find. Let us investigate the interesting field of activities now and see what will best suit the novice and her new pony.

The principal activity is the Working Rally, and these fixtures, of which two or three are held every holiday, are the backbone of the Pony Club. This is generally an all-day rally, members bringing their own packed lunches. Mounted instruction in all phases of riding takes place during the morning, and the afternoon is usually given over to a mock hunt, hunter trial or mounted games. In other words, hard work in the morning and more relaxed enjoyment in the afternoon.

Riders are graded, according to age and ability, so that no one need worry about her inexperience. This is what Pony Club rallies are for and it is here that the novice will find

friends and experts who will help and advise. It is quite remarkable how much a rider can improve in all phases of
horsemanship after an hour or two instruction at a rally.
The ponies improve immensely too, learning to be more responsive and obedient in company with a group of others all
learning the same thing.

In 1932, Tests were devised by Pony Club headquarters,
so that members might prove their knowledge, and they have
done much to stimulate and keep up the standard of horsemanship throughout the Pony Club movement. There are
four Tests, of which the most elementary, Test D, is awarded
for encouragement and keenness. Test C necessitates a
fairly elementary working knowledge of the correct aids in
the different movements, a knowledge of the basic grooming
kit and its various uses and some experience in feeding,
watering and cleanliness of pony and stable. This is not beyond the scope of an enthusiastic novice who has studied this
text and tried to carry out its advice in practice.

Test B and Test A are more advanced and a high standard of equitation is demanded. In fact, the young rider who
passes the Pony Club Test A can regard herself as an extremely competent horsewoman and should qualify for most
jobs with horses open to the young today. There is a school
of thought, at the present time, who feel that this test demands too high a standard. We have not had a member
pass for many years in our local branch, and, yet, we have
some splendid teenage riders. Anyway, it will be a long while
before our beginner to riding need worry about her ability
to pass Test A and we can return to studying horsemanship
at a lower level. These standards do provide an incentive for
members to work towards and no young rider should hesitate
to try to attain them.

Pony Club branch activities include lectures, visits to
Hunt kennels, hunter trials, mounted treks and expeditions,
gymkhanas and summer camps. A glorious selection of interesting events from which the novice and her pony will
benefit immensely. But, remember, when you attend these

fixtures, that all the work done by the long-suffering District Commissioner and her committee is voluntary and they are, probably, very busy people at home, with families to be organised as well as the Pony Club. The helpers, the instructors, the landowners and the farmers are doing a great job for the younger generation and their interest and efforts must be respected. It is through their help alone that thousands of children are being initiated into the love of the horse and pony. Just how we can best show our gratitude to them for what they do, will be described forthwith, when the interesting business of attending Pony Club camp is explored.

The Pony Club now holds four annual inter-branch team championships and although we cannot yet aspire to these ranks, there is no harm in watching what goes on and endeavouring to emulate them. One day our novice will be chosen to represent her branch in some phase of equitation. There are Pony Club Horse Trials, Pony Club Mounted Games, a Pony Club Polo Tournament and a Pony Club Pentathlon.

But the highlight of the Pony Club year for the average member is, undoubtedly, the week that she, or he, spends in camp. It is here, and at the working rallies held during each holiday, that the real spadework of the Pony Club is carried on.

The Camp is divided into senior and junior divisions. The juniors, under eleven or twelve years, this varies in different branches, attend a two or three day fixture, and the seniors have a week. Cost is generally £1 a day, so that the member is, in fact, having a week's holiday for herself and her pony, and tuition, for very little. Some of the larger thriving Pony Club branches, can afford to charge even less. Ponies are either stabled, or kept in lines in the open, and members are housed indoors, or under canvas, or, in this branch, sleeping on camp beds in caravans, trailers and horse boxes. Arrangements, in all branches, will vary according to circumstances, but this gives an idea of what to expect.

The week in camp will consist of tuition in the care of

the horse and regular morning instruction. Afternoons and evenings offer rides, lectures, visits to interesting equine establishments in the district and the last day will mean a gymkhana or hunter trial, held at the camp. Tack cleaning, and grooming, and mucking out, will be supervised, and active help given to beginners in the accomplishment of these fascinating duties.

Camp is always held in August, during school holidays, and novice members without ponies of their own are encouraged to hire their favourites from the riding school in the area which they patronise. Probable cost of hiring a pony for a week will average £10. Sceptical parents should remember, that £20 for a child to enjoy a week's holiday with tuition and exclusive use of a pony, is not excessive and the enjoyment and benefit she will derive will surely be worth every penny.

Attendance at camp will mean conforming to the few rules that have to be made. The hard-working committee are responsible for members during the week, and it does not help to keep affairs running smoothly if children are liable to be unpunctual for meals or to disappear altogether at intervals. Be helpful, and hardworking, and write a letter of thanks, afterwards, to the District Commissioner. These small courtesies are appreciated.

The Pony Club Horse Trials, and Prince Philip Cup Mounted Games for which branches enter teams to qualify for the annual championships, may be beyond the scope of the novice but she will attain these heights in due course. In the meantime, do not miss an opportunity of attending and watching, these events. Study the first class performances which can be seen, and, remember, that riders from the humblest beginnings have reached the top, and will do so again.

Now we come to the movement which has developed more recently than the Pony Club, but which must not be neglected in these pages because it has much to offer the rider of today.

There are now nearly 300 Riding Clubs with a membership of 20,000, affiliated to the British Horse Society. As distinct from the Pony Club, these Clubs are patronised chiefly by adults who may, necessarily, be week-end riders, or people who have left the country for the town and do not wish to lose their connections with horses. Riding Clubs have been formed at universities, hospitals and similar institutions, by business firms and within the armed forces, and some of these clubs are thriving to such a degree that they can afford to own, and support, several horses of their own for the use of their members. Due to these Clubs, the standard of riding in some localities, which would normally not produce any equine talent, is remarkably high. Various annual tests and competitions of different standards are held and there is a keen and friendly spirit of rivalry between the clubs. Scope is wide for Riding Clubs in Britain today, and there is little doubt that they will go from strength to strength and give a lot of pleasure in the saddle to their members who may, or may not, be the owners of horses themselves.

So any young adult who feels that the ranks of the Pony Club are too juvenile for his or her needs, must write to the British Horse Society and find out the headquarters of her nearest Riding Club. The fact that the members may be chiefly week-end, or holiday riders, does not seem to have rendered the movement any less powerful. A vast public have now been introduced to riding who would not, thirty years ago, have got further than the fringe of the horse world.

CHAPTER TWELVE

FOXHUNTING

What is the fascination that foxhunting holds, for so many people who ride, and enjoy horses – what is there in it for the young, and if we get a taste for it, what has it got to offer to a keen young rider?

Foxhunting was wont to be regarded as a sport for the rich, and the well-to-do, and we hear from those who are against it, that the future of hunting is in jeopardy. Actually, more people hunt today than ever before, hounds are faster and more scientifically hunted and the horses ridden in the chase are of better quality than heretofore. Motor transport has helped the lot of the hunting man considerably and his comfort, and that of his mount have been greatly increased because of it.

It is true, alas, that almost all hunting country has deteriorated and every change in political, and consequently agricultural policy, has affected sport, past and present. Today, with many more small owners of land, there is, not unnaturally, a diversity of ideas as to how to bolster up the agricultural industry. This has led to many experiments, some of them far from helpful to sport. Agricultural labour, despite modern inventions, is less skilled and higher paid. Drainage is not always adequate, in many places ditches have not been cleaned out for years, hedges have been allowed to run riot or have been done away with altogether to save labour. Barbed wire has been everywhere erected for the same reason. In addition, the country to be ridden over has been curtailed by thousands of acres. That the Midlands are becoming more industrialised is understandable but they are not more adversely affected than many of the provincial hunts.

Artificial fertilisers, modern highways and not least, the

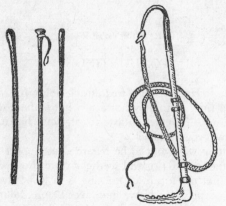

Fig. 21. Riding canes – hunting whip

ever-increasing number of car followers at every meet do hinder scent, but on the credit side, the Hunt Supporters' Clubs are flourishing and these same car followers bring welcome revenue into the Hunt Fund.

Young people from every walk of life are now seen out with hounds and it is quite certain that our beginner, who will now be becoming competent, and looking about for some more sport, will be interested in what her local pack of hounds has to offer.

First, what will it cost to hunt? Apart from a little extra food for the pony during the season, and the need to pay someone to trace-clip him, the chief expense will be the hunt subscription. This varies in different areas, but the average is now £50 per horse each season for an adult hunting member. Teenage children or rather their parents, are expected to contribute a small share as well. This is just as it should be, although, unfortunately, not all parents of riding children seem able to appreciate this fact. Consider that these young-sters have just as much sport as their elders and probably do just as much damage to fences. No one can go ice-skating, or to the swimming baths, or even for an hour to the cinema,

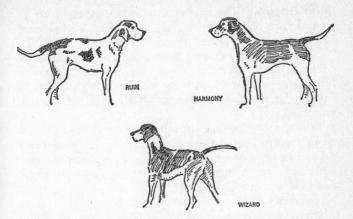

RUIN

HARMONY

WIZARD

Fig. 22. The beginner will be interested in what the local
pack of hounds has to offer

without being expected to pay for it, so why should they
feel free to gallop over other people's fields, and fences, behind an expensively maintained pack of hounds, for nothing.

The opening meet of the season is held during the first
week in November and for two months before this, cub-
hunting will have been going on. The purpose of cub-hunting is to teach the young hounds the rudiments of the game
and to break up the litters of cubs just as they are becoming
old enough to become a nuisance to the local farmers. In
addition, hunt horses, who have enjoyed three months at
grass, must be got fit for the season.

Cub-hunting takes place very early in the morning, or,
rather, it commences at the crack of dawn, but will not finish
until mid morning. It means having the pony in his stable all
night and everything laid in readiness for an early start.
But the few hours out with hounds will be excellent training
for the young rider being introduced to hounds and hunting.
It is delightful on a misty September morning to stand outside a covert and listen to hounds hunting about amongst

the undergrowth. This is when they must learn to answer to various notes on the horn, to hunt young foxes and to leave rabbits and hares alone. There will be cobwebs on the brambles and leaves floating down from the branches of the trees and possibly even a nip of frost in the air. There is truly little to compare with the early morning delights of autumn, in woodland and countryside, on a cub-hunting morning.

In November, hunting starts in earnest and before we set off up the first field at a spanking pace, with our pony's ears pricked and our own thoughts fixed upon the tempting post and rails over which we are planning to sail, we must look first to those in authority in the hunting field.

Nowadays, many packs of hounds have two or three Masters, called Joint-Masters. Possibly the Master may hunt hounds or he may engage a professional man to do the job. There is also a Whip, who is the huntsman's right-hand man, and he has a variety of tasks to perform. Somehow, he is expected to view the fox away, round up stray hounds, negotiate any obstacles that confront him in the execution of these tasks, and be in at the kill. There is also a Field Master who is responsible for controlling the mounted company present. In these ranks will be found our enthusiastic novice, and her pony, and so it is to the Field Master that she will chiefly look for guidance. He does not appreciate riders who gallop about unnecessarily or override hounds.

Never let your pony kick a hound, or get in the way of the officials in the execution of their duties. It is surprising how many ignorant young riders do stand about in narrow lanes, and in gateways, so that the Whip can scarcely push his way past. Always open a gate for older mounted followers, and take care to shut it again if you are the last rider through. Growing seeds must be respected, and not galloped over, and any broken fence reported to the Secretary of the hunt, to whom, by the way, you will already have given your 'cap' or day's hunt subscription at the meet.

It should always be remembered that hunting is only

carried out by the farmers' kindness in letting hounds hunt over their land. So it is important not to leave gates unlatched, so that stock may stray, and not face your pony at fences which are too big for him and which he will inevitably smash in an endeavour to get over. The idea out hunting is not to gallop about showing off in front of friends and causing your pony to sweat with exhaustion early in the day. Far better to take an intelligent interest in what hounds are doing and to watch, and learn, from the more experienced mounted members of the hunt.

It is useful for the young rider to hounds to find herself a pilot, whom she can follow with confidence. What do we look for in such a mentor, and friend, or perhaps, it might be easier to know what to avoid.

The man or woman who, whilst riding hard, takes too much out of his horse and does not know what hounds are doing will be said to have 'no eye for a country'. He is constantly galloping about, but never seems able to keep with hounds, and by using his heels to make up for the deficiency in intellect, he will in time wear down the best of horses, and the most faithful young follower. This type are inclined to be voluble, and to make up in noise, and bluster what they lack in nerve.

There are also followers who neither pretend to, nor do, ride up to hounds, because from insufficiency of nerve, old age, or being badly mounted, they are unable to. They are, as a rule, keen sportsmen and infinitely preferable companions to those who always come up an hour after the kill, with numerous excuses why they were not in at the finish.

There is one class of rider to hounds who is positively dangerous, not only to those in whose company they ride, but also to the best interests of hunting. Watch out for these people and never try to emulate them.

Their favourite trick is to ride on your horse's heels, and there is no more unpleasant sensation, than to be aware that a rider is coming close behind you, for if your pony makes a mistake, the other fellow is bound to be on top of you. So never be guilty of doing this yourself. Another annoying trick is to persist in riding at a fence at which you have just refused several times, thereby effectively blocking the way for the rest of the field who are waiting for a turn. In these days of wire fences and made-up jumps there is seldom room for more than two, at most, to ride abreast at a jump. If one rider has already refused several times, with his mount swerving away from the fence broadside on, the rest of the field are likely to lose the hunt and possibly sustain injury by remaining at this fence.

It is hoped that the above may help our novice to recognise the base from the true metal, and that it will help her pick out the real hunting folk who are always quietly up with hounds, real professors of the art, a few of whom may be found in every hunt.

As we learn to know the neighbouring country by hacking around it during summer months, so our pupil will know, too, of many gaps, gates and small fences which her pony can comfortably negotiate. It is important to take advantage of short cuts, when mounted on a pony, as he will tire before his larger brethren, and must be spared as much as possible when he begins to do so. At the end of a run, if the novice has kept up and is in at the kill, or a lengthy check, she should dismount and loosen her pony's girths and walk him about to cool off. Do not forget to draw them up when you mount again. It is not etiquette to sit on a sweating pony telling friends how fast you went and what big fences you have jumped.

It is not necessary to be elaborately equipped for hunting. Nevertheless, it is for all of us, within the range of our pockets, to dress as well as we can out of compliment to the Master and to the Hunt. Be clean, and as well turned out as you can manage to be.

Tweed jacket, jodhpurs and a hard hat are adequate. But for a rider over fifteen years, who hopes to hunt fairly regularly, a pair of hunting boots and breeches would be a wise investment. Well-fitting boots are so much more comfortable than anything else for a long day in the saddle and they look very elegant. A navy, or black coat worn with a stock is also correct, and the jacket will also be useful for showing. A new coat would cost £25 or thereabouts but it should be possible to find a second-hand one for much less.

When the rider turns her pony's head for home, with the new boots mud-splashed and the white stock slightly awry, she must be sure to walk or trot slowly back. If two friends return together it should not become a trotting marathon. The pony needs to come home relaxed and cool. There is a pleasurable feeling anyway, about hacking home with a companion, both ponies tired and looking forward to a warm stable and a meal and their riders to a hot bath and a hearty tea.

Before we can indulge in our own comforts, however, our pony's needs must be attended to on arrival home. Call at the house, and report a safe return to the parents, but leave the details of the day to be enlarged upon later in the evening. Strip the tack off the pony, let him shake himself, and drink, and then rub him down with a wisp. Girth marks, ears and under the belly will be particularly damp and sweaty. Examine his legs for thorns and pick out his hooves for stones which may have become wedged in during the day.

If the pony lives out, which he probably will do, if he is kept at home, he may be turned out into the field as soon as he is dry. He will love a good roll after the day's exertions. A pony kept at a riding school will stay in and there will be no lack of willing helpers to unsaddle him, rub him down, and to listen enviously to descriptions of the day's activities.

By the way, children who can afford to keep their ponies at riding schools are fortunate during the hunting season, because there are generally one or two riders going from the establishment, and so transport will be arranged, and our pupil can avail herself of a lift to the meet. There will also be friends to go along with during the day.

The morning after hunting it is better not to take the pony out riding, or at least not very far, and certainly no schooling, or jumping practice, unless the hunting had been a very short day. If he is not a very young pony, he may be stiff, so lead him out for a walk, and let him graze the grass verges or the road for twenty minutes. He will enjoy the sweet young grass as a change from his paddock.

CHAPTER THIRTEEN

GYMKHANA AND HORSE SHOWS. PRACTISING
AT HOME FOR THESE, AND PROCEDURE ON
THE DAY

Having enjoyed some exciting days with hounds during
winter months, our beginner will be becoming even more
ambitious as spring and summer come round again. Everyone interested in horses and ponies will have, already, either
visited a horse show or a gymkhana or have watched show
jumping on television. Now that she possesses a mount of
her own and is coming to better terms with him as each
week goes by, so our pupil begins to wonder whether they
might not try something of this nature themselves.

Better not be too ambitious to start with. Show jumping
really is a little beyond our scope at the moment. But riding
in gymkhanas and at smaller shows is not, so we must investigate what they have to offer the amateur.

A gymkhana is really a festival of mounted games. Nowadays the officials usually include a jumping class and a handy
pony class to raise the tone and draw the crowds, but everything is on a lesser scale than the large agricultural, and
horse shows, and is intended to attract beginners as well as
more experienced riders. Gymkhanas are great fun to take
part in and admirably suited to our beginner and her pony,
and their capabilities.

Some gymkhanas are held in conjunction with village
fêtes, or are arranged by the local Pony Club branch or
may simply be organised by a few horsey enthusiasts in the
district. They can be very impromptu affairs with only
rosettes for prizes but, nonetheless, fun for the competitors.
Although it is nice to win, with a few exceptions no one
minds terribly if they don't, though everyone tries desper-
ately hard to do so. During the games, ponies can be pulled

about unnecessarily roughly in the enthusiasm of the moment, bridles have even been pulled right over their ears in their riders' efforts to tow them along in the sack race, or similar, and saddles are always slipping about their owner's backs. So try not to be too rough in the heat of the moment and respect your pony's dignity even if he is being rather stubborn and slow.

Before going to a gymkhana quite a lot of practising can be done at home. Events will include a bending race, musical posts, obstacle race and a potato race and basically all these events are the same and simply require a degree of handiness and speed. In other words we must get to work schooling hard in the paddock and practising the aids. Thus we should learn to guide the pony with legs and body and not by hauling him around by the reins and vigorous use of the heels.

Get some posts or bamboo canes and drive them firmly into the ground in your paddock, at equal distances apart. Practise bending in and out of these at the trot and at the canter. This is splendid practice, both for the bending race and for other games too. Take a bucket out into the field and some potatoes, and having ridden between the bending posts make the pony halt at the bucket placed at the end of the line and lean down and drop each potato in. It is surprising how much more difficult this is than it sounds. Some ponies will not stand still, others object to the rattle and it is as well to get him accustomed to all this now, before the gymkhana. Otherwise, it will be frustrating if he will not co-operate and backs away at sight of the bucket. Practise riding in circles at a hand canter and turning sharply using legs and body and not too much hauling on the reins. This will be useful for musical posts.

In a handy pony class, presentation, and looks, do count quite a bit, but even if the pony is at a disadvantage regarding looks, quite a lot can be done to school him to the required standard. He will gain marks for standing quietly whilst being mounted, for reining back correctly and for jumping a small fence. Careful grooming and cleaning of tack beforehand will also help. These handy pony classes are admirable training for novice riders and their ponies and it is a pity that gymkhana organisers do not always include them in their schedules. Being rather slow work to judge and not a spectacular class for spectators, fast races and jumping classes are regarded as better crowd attractions.

Graduating to small horse shows, or the pony classes held in conjunction with the agricultural shows, we must carefully study the schedule of classes offered, before making an entry. It is surprising how many show secretaries have to return incorrectly filled-in forms to would-be competitors. How tiresome this must be for the already over-worked secretary. So do read the various conditions in the entry form carefully and write clearly when making an entry. You may not be sure exactly how high your pony stands, and which class he will be eligible for. The nearest riding school will have a measuring stick and will be able to advise about entries, and may have a fair idea what competition there would be in the various classes for a novice.

Practise schooling in circles at home and, if possible, persuade brothers and sisters, or friends, to stand around the home-made circle and shout and wave handkerchiefs, to get the pony accustomed to crowd behaviour. Remember to school in both directions in the circle, so that the pony does not get accustomed to always leading on the right fore leg which it may be his natural tendency to do.

Teach the pony to run in-hand. This means dismounting, running the stirrup irons up the leathers and removing the saddle, placing it on the ground behind the pony and well away from the others. The saddle should be placed upright and not thrown down carelessly. Now bring the reins over the pony's head and stand holding him at his near side shoulder, right hand holding the reins short behind his chin and left hand holding up the long loop of rein.

At a signal from the judge or the ring steward that the previous pony has finished his display, our pupil will lead her pony out, and, standing facing him, will make him stand for the judge to look him over. Then he must be walked up a short distance and trotted back. Walk level with his shoulder, never drag him and look back at him, and when turning round, push him away from you rather than dragging him round. It makes a big difference if he will walk and trot out freely on the run in-hand, and does not need shooing by the steward. Practise this a lot at home and get a friend to come behind, if necessary, and hurry him up, until he learns that you mean business.

The idea of the run in-hand is so that the judge can see the pony stripped. Saddles can conceal minor defects in conformation and he can also judge better whether the pony's action is quite straight.

Preparation for the show will be intense and it is as well to start getting ready several days beforehand. Although good looks are, alas, all-important and our beginner's pony may not be much of a looker, presentation of the animal counts a lot. So he must be clean and fit and well shod and well behaved. Quite a challenge for a novice rider.

Clean all tack thoroughly the day before the show. Clean all your riding clothes too, polish shoes or jodhpur boots, brush the jacket and find a clean shirt and a large clean handkerchief. Never leave these jobs to be done on the morning of the show, there will be plenty of other things to see to regarding the pony's personal appearance.

The night before the show it would be wise to keep the pony in his stable overnight, otherwise he will be sure to roll in his field and have some nice damp muddy patches on his coat. If there is no stable, leave him out and hope for the best. Grey ponies can collect some nasty yellow stains by lying down on their bedding in the box, anyway, and this can be just as bad. So it may be a choice of two evils.

Get up early and groom the pony thoroughly before breakfast. Brush out the tail and mane, it can make a tremendous difference. A plaited mane does look very smart,

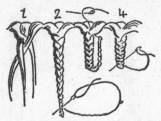

Fig. 23. The four stages of plaiting

seven plaits is the usual number and coloured wool or thread should not be used. But plaiting is no job for a novice, she will have to have some instruction in the art from an expert before she can do it with any skill, so leave the mane as nature intended it to be this morning. A little trimming around the pony's fetlocks and pasterns could be done, but too much hair should not be taken away, because this acts as a natural protection against mud and wet for the legs and hooves.

Sponge the pony's eyes and nostrils and finally paint his hooves with Neat's foot oil. By this time he should be looking really splendid. The time has come to have a good breakfast yourself and to change into the garments laid in readiness. Check each item carefully, because the day will be quite spoilt if you arrive at the show and find that you have forgotten to put your hat on or have left your packet of sandwiches on the kitchen table. Although we shall hope that the family will have been filled with enthusiasm too and are bringing a large picnic lunch in the car to sustain their young hopeful.

Tack up the pony now, and put his headcollar or halter over the bridle, and if you are riding to the show, knot the rope around his neck. Otherwise, if he is travelling in a horse-box this rope will be needed to tether him inside.

Having reached the showground, unload the pony, and find the correct place to tie him up. We shall hope it will be a nice shady spot. There will be lots to see, and friends to

Fig. 24. Tail pulled – natural tail

talk to, but go straight to the secretary's tent and get your number and find out what time your class is likely to come up.

Now it will be quite legitimate to mount and ride around the show ground. This should help to accustom the pony to the many strange sights and sounds before he must go in the main ring. Do not show off by galloping about in front of envious dismounted friends, and never ride too near spectators and small children. They are just as important as the riders and do not appreciate being mud-spattered or over-ridden. Without the paying public there would be no shows to compete in so we must respect them and be grateful that they feel it worth coming to see us.

As time draws near for the class, proceed to the collecting ring and walk quietly round inside. Keep the pony going well into his bridle and listen to what the steward is saying. Once in the collecting ring, riders have placed themselves voluntarily under the jurisdiction of the ring steward, so any instructions issued by him must be obeyed.

Now, at last we are entering the main ring, try not to follow closely behind the best looking pony in the class, but, all the same, get in one of the first few if this can be managed, without any pushing or shoving. First impressions do count, so let them be favourable ones. Keep the pony walking out freely, head up and neck nicely arched and your own hands down and back straight. Refrain from grinning or waving cheerily to friends at the ringside and never ride too close to the pony in front or ride bunched up in a crowd of other ponies.

The stewards will indicate when the competitors must trot and canter on and when the signal is given, it is not the start of a race. Move on at a collected pace, encouraging the pony to make a smooth transition from one pace to another. When the ponies are called in, and whilst each is being ridden out to give a show, make your pony stand alert, not resting a hindleg and drooping his head. If he is fidgety, this is much more awkward. Try not to get flustered but dismount and hold him if he persists in shifting around to the extent of annoying his neighbours.

Not every competitor is always asked to lead his pony out in-hand or to ride out and give a show. Particularly if the class is a big one. If you have to do this, make the most of it. Walk him up and down as he has been taught and then ride a simple figure of eight at a trot and then at a canter. Not too long or elaborate a show as it is a pity to spoil your chances by attempting too much, and doing the whole badly, or boring the judge with your performance.

When the final choice for the coveted rosettes is made, it will be an enormous thrill if our pupil finds herself, and her pony, among the ribbons. Thank the judge who presents the rosette and he, or a steward, will pin it on the pony's bridle. No words could be written to describe the pride and pleasure of this moment. We shall hope our novice will experience it for herself without just having to read about it.

Try not to mind if your pony did not quite match up to the others and was relegated to the also-rans. It is dispiriting after all the hard work, but it has been a lot of fun and a wonderful new experience. Only a few ponies can win, and there are so many dedicated people about now who take this showing business in deadly earnest, that it isn't easy for the novice to keep up with them. There are some lovely ponies in the show rings, beautifully presented and ridden, but if our own pony has behaved himself, and looked smart, he will still have been a credit, and a source of great pride to his owner.

CHAPTER FOURTEEN

SHOW JUMPING

It is strange that show organisers all over the country are being faced with increasing entries in all horse events and declining gates. In other words, more people than ever wish to compete, but, now, not so many will come to watch. Preferring perhaps to stay at home and see the events, or some of them, on television. A problem, indeed, for the organisers. Many of the smaller agricultural shows are grinding to a halt because of lack of support from the public. But the competitors are still eager to participate, despite the fact that prize money is not large at the smaller shows.

There is no doubt that the atmosphere of showing is unique and tremendously exciting. For many people the game has become a hobby and they love it and spend all the summer months at it. These folk do keep showing very much alive, but they also make it rather difficult for the genuine amateur who is trying to make a way up from scratch.

Show jumping has become very professional, although perhaps there is more scope here for the novice because there are lots and lots of shows, all over the country, who do still have jumping classes and it doesn't matter at all what the pony looks like, or how he is bred, in these classes. All that matters is that he can show a clean pair of heels over the sticks, and this is where the hard working rider, who schools her pony industriously for many weeks at home, will score.

Anyone who has ever made a name in show jumping, has spent many hours behind the scenes with a rigorous training programme.

It is one thing to jump over a variety of natural looking obstacles during the course of the morning ride, and quite another to face the pony at a brightly painted collection of fences in the show ring. So we must get busy in the home paddock with a paint brush, and a willing helper, preferably male, who is also a good amateur carpenter.

Cavalletti, which our novice already possesses, can be painted white, and poles can be painted red and white. An old door, disguised with a coat of paint makes an excellent imitation wall. Straw bales are also most useful for wings and even as jumps themselves, two or three set lengthways. Sheep hurdles, tree branches and oil drums also make good accessories.

Before beginning to school the pony to show jump, it is extremely helpful to watch jumping competitions where experts are competing. Do not merely admire the look of the horse, and there are some jolly good-lookers among the show jumpers, and idly tot up the points lost on each round. Concentrate upon the rider's style and tactics, all the professionals have their own, and really study exactly why a horse goes wrong. Time spent in this way will not be wasted. Many performances are far from perfect but even from them there is something to be learnt.

If you can persuade someone to photograph you jumping your small obstacles in the paddock this would be invaluable. Then you can see yourself clearly, for once, as others see you.

Learning to show jump is not galloping madly at the new jumps without any warning the first morning that they are completed. If the pony is in the right frame of mind he may hop obligingly over the resplendent objects but more likely he may refuse, or run out, and get tired of it all before we have begun. Much better take things slowly for a week or two. Rider and pony will have already done a certain amount of jumping over the cavalletti, and small jumps encountered during rides, so that they will be accustomed to the movement. Now after ten minutes schooling and practising the aids, and acquiring a nice measure of balance together, the next thing to be done is to ride the pony up to each obstacle at a walk and let him have a good look.

Then put two of them down very low and trot up to them and let him go over easily so that he gains confidence and does not have his mouth hurt. Gradually, other jumps can be attempted and the height slightly raised. This work is better carried out after coming in from your ride as the pony will be much more supple and responsive than when he has just been mounted. Horses have their own ways of overcoming obstacles and some like to get uncomfortably close to the fence before taking off. This can be very unseating, especially if the pony likes to make a slow approach, but can be improved by placing a pole on the ground on the take off side.

Should the pony begin to rush things and want to gallop in as soon as he is turned towards an obstacle, we must go more slowly and prevent this habit becoming worse. He either does it because he has become over-excited, and flustered, or merely because he loves the game and wants to have a fling. Too much speed going into the jump can spell disaster, and spills, and flattened fences, and this state of affairs must be avoided at all costs.

The use of the whip or cane by children in the show jumping ring has led to much controversy and criticism in recent years. Whipping a pony when he refuses an obstacle is, of course, quite wrong, but a stubborn old pony who jumps perfectly well at home, or when he happens to be feeling like it, will take no harm from a sharp rap either on the rump or down the shoulder, as he comes into the fence.

So far, the procedure sounds quite simple and we hope that everything will turn out to be so. But of course it is not at all easy. If the rider is progressing well, her pony is responding to the training and she is beginning to study schedules for show jumping classes, in earnest, then it would be wise to organise some jumping lessons at a good riding school or equitation centre, if you are lucky enough to have one near. It is so easy to write down what the novice should, and should not do, but things do not always work out as they should, in practice, because ponies all differ and they are unpredictable animals anyway.

So do go ahead and arrange a course of jumping lessons,

because the experience gained for pony and rider will be invaluable. Cost for a private lesson may be a guinea, or more, but it will be worth it. I would suggest two private jumping lessons and a course of six lessons, with a group. Cost of the latter will be, approximately, 52½p a lesson.

Imagine how helpful this is going to be. One or two small jumps, made from cavaletti will be set up in the school, and there will be an instructor to tell you exactly what to do, and to point out any faults in style you may have collected, and which are difficult to recognise and to eradicate working alone. The pony will be much more responsive in an enclosed school and more inclined to keep his mind on the job.

Depending upon the size of the pony, so it will depend which class you enter him for. Maximum height for 14.2 h.h. ponies is usually four feet, three feet nine inches for 13.2 h.h. and three feet six inches for 12.2. So this gives an indication of what you have to aim at.

As work progresses, cavaletti and other obstacles should be gradually raised as balance improves. Cavaletti may also be placed in pairs directly behind each other and at a low height. This will give a good spread, teaching the pony to stretch out head and neck and to use his natural jumping ability to the fullest extent. The pole placed on the take-off side for the pony who gets too close to his jumps, can also be moved slightly in and out. So he will learn to look at the bottom of the obstacle, and not the top as he approaches, and this will help him to judge more accurately the extent of his leap.

Apart from some small competitions at minor shows and gymkhanas, practically all show jumping is now under the jurisdiction of the British Show Jumping Association. Shows and competitors must all abide by the rules laid down. The country is divided into areas, each of which has its own representative, whose duty it is to keep in touch with the executives of all shows in their areas. There are also rules laid down by the B.S.J.A. for courses, and types of jumps, with permitted heights and spreads, and suggested time limits.

If the pony has already been to some gymkhanas or has been entered in handy pony classes he will have become accustomed already to the atmosphere of a show and the attendant noise and bustle. His rider will know the routine when she arrives on the showground.

When collecting the number from the secretary's tent it is helpful to enquire the order of jumping because if there are a lot of entries this could save a lot of standing about waiting in the collecting ring. Should the pony benefit from a practise jump before his competition there is sure to be one erected somewhere on the field. Different ponies require varied periods of work before jumping and how much, or how little, can be ascertained as the rider learns to know her pony and his ways. The thing we want to ensure is that he is alert and in an obedient frame of mind.

Then it will be time to ride into the ring and inspect the fences. Most shows insist on this being done dismounted and many show jumpers prefer this anyway. But our novice will be wise to take her pony into the ring, if she is allowed to, because the show will, necessarily, only be a minor one as yet, and the pony would benefit from this. As the majority of shows wage a continual fight against time, it is customary for only a short time to be allowed for competitors to inspect the course. So do not spend too long gazing at the first, or chatting merrily to a friend, but ride around looking closely at each obstacle, trying to judge distances between fences, and the number of strides likely to be needed. Make quite certain that you know the route to take and if in doubt about anything ask a steward for advice. They are there to help competitors.

There is an old saying applied to jumping which indicates that we should 'throw our hearts over the fence first' and the rest will automatically follow. Well, there is something in this idea of a bold approach. Nerves communicate themselves to horses and a bold confident approach to the first fence will make the pony feel that his rider, at least, is determined to get to the other side. Apprehension about the pony refusing may quite well make him do so. Some horses enjoy showing-off and actually jump better in competitions than they do at home. Others, alas, can be very tiresome and this is particularly true of ponies, who in many instances have more intelligence than their larger kind. Disappointed children at gymkhana and Pony Club events can be heard bemoaning the sad fact that their ponies jump beautifully, alone in the field at home, but will not go near the jumps when it comes to a competition.

So on entering the show ring for the start of our jumping round we must ride calmly and with great determination. This will be the test of all the training and preparation. If you do incure a refusal do not go too far back for a long run in before having a second attempt. Keep looking ahead all the time, and, even if you have touched a pole, do not look back. Once over one fence all attention should be focused upon the next and how best to negotiate it together.

How thrilling it will be to hear the commentator announce 'clear round' as the pair of you ride out of the ring together. There will certainly be applause from round the ring. Success may not be ours as yet but it is certainly within our grasp.

Dismount immediately, loosen the pony's girths and lead him quietly about in hand, whilst keeping one eye upon the fortunes of the other competitors in the ring. There will almost certainly be other clear rounds, so there will have to be a jump-off.

A jump-off means that the obstacles will be heightened and in some cases the spreads enlarged. The pony, however, having had one clear round will go round with aplomb and there should be no question of worrying about refusals if our novice has got this far. She can scarcely, in fact, now be correctly termed a novice. Great care must be taken not to be careless in this round because this is when poles and bricks roll out of place and points are lost. Success in the first round must not overshadow necessary caution and precision in the second. Ride with determination and intelligence and, we hope, the prize will be won.

Now, I think, we can allow ourselves a feeling of tremendous achievement and congratulations from friends can be acknowledged and enjoyed. Probably a collected canter in triumph round the ring will be the next item, not a mad gallop, by the way, with the rosette fluttering proudly on the bridle. Other prize winners will follow round the ring and thus all the spectators get a close view of the winners.

After this triumph, return to the box, unsaddle and rub the pony down. Give him a drink and leave him to graze tied up, if possible, in the shade.

Of course we may not have been quite as successful as we had hoped, in fact, rosettes and honours cannot really be expected to come our way for quite a while. But they will come, in the end, if the rider and pony train hard together and there will be plenty of other good days to come at other shows.

CHAPTER FIFTEEN

THE BRITISH HORSE SOCIETY. DESCRIPTION OF THE CENTRE AT KENILWORTH. VARIOUS EQUESTRIAN EVENTS

For many years the British Horse Society, the British Show Jumping Association and the Pony Club had been conducting business from increasingly overcrowded offices at Bedford Square, London. As interest in the horse revived after the last war, so the premises became more uncomfortable and cramped and it became progressively more difficult to efficiently house the country's entire administrative complex of equestrian organisations and stores. Officials of the societies began to realise that a move might have to be made although the daunting prospect of finding somewhere, suitable and central, put off the decision for some years.

Then, in 1965, a site was offered by the Royal Agricultural Society, of a plot of land on their permanent show ground at Stoneleigh, Kenilworth, Warwickshire. A committee was formed to investigate this interesting offer and it was found to be an ideal situation for the necessary offices and for a riding school. So the idea of a National Equestrian Centre at Stoneleigh was born and the last five years have seen a dream realised and a development of major importance taking place in the horse world of Great Britain.

The British Horse Society is recognised by our government as the national body responsible for equitation. As well as furthering the interests of horsemen and women in general the society also aims to encourage the improvement and expansion of good riding facilities all over the country. Great Britain has reached the top of the tree in equestrian sport and the society has shouldered responsibility for selecting and training teams to represent the country in international horse shows and competitions.

The National Equestrian Centre is worth a visit to any young person seriously interested in the welfare of the horse, and visitors are made welcome and the diverse equestrian activities taking place there can be more readily understood. The largest covered riding school in the country has been erected near the offices and there should not fail to be a steady improvement in the standard of riding. Good instructors are still a problem in many branches of riding clubs and pony clubs but courses are being organised at the centre to endeavour to overcome this.

Visiting the centre, one is immediately struck by the air of efficiency and helpfulness. There is already a library, a lecture room, a canteen and a conference room with a bar. The school itself is made very attractive by large blown up photographs of the pony breeds mounted on a panel along one wall. Various Hunts in Great Britain have taken glass panels in the arcade outside with their names on them. Seats in the gallery have been contributed by Pony Club branches from all over the world and the respective seats will have the name of the branch attached to them. So various organisations in the horse world can feel that they have a hand in the development of this centre and many trade organisations have contributed very generously in cash, and in kind.

The ultimate aim behind the indoor riding school, the cross-country course, the outside ménage and, later, the stables to be built at Stoneleigh, is to provide a university for teaching riding and horse management. It does not seek in any way, and officials of the centre stress this point, to compete with the many excellent riding schools and equitation centres which already exist in the country.

There is a national instructor at the centre and the fee for a private lesson from him, to a member in the riding school for an hour, is £2. An individual lesson from the assistant instructor is £1. Local riding clubs and pony club branches may hire the school for £2 an hour. Even the fences in the school may be hired for an hour for 50p. Various interesting lectures for members are held on such diverse subjects as, showing, pony trekking holidays, judging and veterinary subjects.

So, if our reader lives within reach of Kenilworth in Warwickshire she can consider herself as very fortunate. But even if she does not, the British Horse Society seems to be a very worthwhile organisation for an aspiring young horseman or woman to join.

During practically every month in the year, there are interesting equestrian activities taking place in various forms all over the country. Point-to-points, combined training events and hunter trials, shows and gymkhanas. Enormous enjoyment can be got out of a day with horses in these diverse forms and much can be learnt by an astute amateur.

The local point-to-point is an interesting day out for the amateur horseman. It is a source of discussion and expectancy for weeks beforehand and is a meeting place and gathering of congenial friends from all the neighbouring hunts.

As the end of each hunting season draws near, the thoughts of the hunting man and woman turn towards the various point-to-points to be held in the locality. It is natural that the desire should be evident to try out the good horse which has gone consistently well behind hounds all season. Unfortunately, many hitherto natural courses have become very much of the galloping type. Such as brush fences which are neither stiff nor high and which even a sketchy jumper can negotiate. But in these days it does need jockeyship as well as boldness to win races, and point-to-points are often a stepping stone to fame under National Hunt rules.

Watching these races today the spectator may be certain that every animal she is watching has had many weeks of definite preparation and every jockey is fit and has done some schooling. Study the horses, how splendidly muscled up and fit they are and how much they are enjoying the work.

The point-to-point also brings in very welcome revenue to the hunt, where every pack is needing funds to ensure survival. Entry to the field is free for spectators, but cars are charged anything from 50p to £2 for use of the car parks. As not many people can get to a meeting without a car, and race cards are sold at 12½p or 15p and we cannot enjoy the afternoon without one, the hunt generally nets a fairly substantial profit.

Although these races have changed in many ways since they started, this in no way takes away from their value. Friendly rivalry is still displayed, especially in the members' and local farmers' races.

A few tips for the visitor to the local Hunt races might be welcome here. Do remember to take a shooting stick, not just for these events but for all horsey fixtures you may patronise. Do consider that many horses hate crowds at the jumps so stand back and encourage others to do the same. Loose dogs are quite definitely forbidden. If you want to lay a bet, do not always choose your horse by its rider, have a look at the horse too! Also, refrain from boring knowledgeable friends by asking for tips. Remember to take a pencil for marking the race card and hot soup or hot coffee for revival. Point-to-points can be perishing affairs.

Hunter trials are becoming increasingly popular events and are more within the scope of the amateur today than either point-to-point riding or combined training events. The latter, more commonly, perhaps, described as 'horse trials' have become very high class.

Hunter trials seem to supply the connecting link between jumping competitions held under B.S.J.A. rules, and the top speed point-to-point races. Furthermore, they have been instrumental in raising the standard of training and performance of the average hunter. Perhaps more of these events would be organised but climatic conditions in spring and autumn when they take place, make the risk of incurring financial loss a considerable one as they do not seem to have the spectator appeal that point-to-point racing offers. Moreover, unless very good natural facilities exist, the building of a suitable course, or courses, entails considerable trouble and expense.

The hunter trial course will be as natural as possible and typical of the country in which the trials are being held. So, if our novice has a horse, or pony, which displays natural jumping ability, and both have had some experience jumping out hunting, there is no reason at all why she may not put in an entry at the local hunter trials. Style of jumping will receive due consideration in the marking, the horse or pony which negotiates his fences clearly and in a well-balanced and collected style receiving more points than the one which gets over anyhow, without actually hitting them.

The fences will be solidly constructed as they must be of sufficient strength to permit of a large number of horses performing over them without becoming unduly battered. This should not deter our novice's pony who will be likely to prefer a natural timber fence to the painted combinations he will encounter in the show jumping ring.

A guiding rule for hunter trial course managers is not to make the mistake of arranging too many classes. If it is a good course to ride over, and there are valuable prizes, there will be no shortage of entries. In this case, it is better to have fewer classes and to get them run off punctually, but without undue rush and hurry, than to have the proceedings scrambled through in order to get them finished before dark.

The pair class makes a good start for the novice rider. If she can persuade a more experienced rider to go round with her in this class she should get a good gallop round. This will be grand experience for herself and her mount.

Hunter trials are now widely held by the Pony Club branches. It is a matter of some difficulty to the organisers to construct courses which will be fair and suitable to all concerned. Children up to the age of seventeen vary so tremendously in their capabilities and the size of the horses and ponies. The commonest method of judging at these trials is to enlist the help of members' parents to stand at a jump and mark all competitors over them. Score sheets are then gathered in at the end of each class. This does ensure that every competitor is marked by the same judge over the same obstacles. As parents and friends without a great deal of horse knowledge can quite well cope with this, because there is generally a simple system of marking, the novice rider should be able to promote her family in this way and thus their interest in and sympathy for, her hobby will be stimulated.

Combined training events are most interesting and thrilling fixtures. Should our beginner ever reach the heights of competing in one of these competitions, she can feel herself a horsewoman of ability. Horse trials, as these fixtures are sometimes more flippantly called, are held in the form of One-day events or Three-day events. The Pony Club Inter-branch competition is held on these lines and the Riding Clubs are arranging similar fixtures; riders being expected to complete three phases – dressage, cross-country riding and jumping.

The object of this test is to find riders and horses who are versatile enough to have reached a high standard in these three varied spheres of horsemanship. Dressage will, if correctly carried out, improve a horse's jumping and over-all obedience, because it is, in fact, simply the applying of the basic aids to a better standard of perfection.

The cross-country phase is tremendous fun to compete in and has especial appeal to the young rider who enjoys riding cross-country behind hounds. Courses are built to conform to the contours of the country and, thus, may include steep banks, thickly wooded rides, wide brooks or streams with stony or slippery take-offs and open walls and timber fences. An exciting challenge to any active rider who is fortunate enough to possess a naturally good jumper.

Combined training events are expensive to organise, because they do not seem to attract spectators as readily as shows. In order to see a majority of obstacles on a cross-country course it may be necessary to walk a mile and a half through wet grass or even mud. Also, the average spectator may be interested in watching one or two dressage tests, but not twenty or thirty, and during the course of the morning there may be nothing else going on. An excellent system of commentating is arranged at the larger trials and efforts are being made to improve all facilities at these fixtures.

Visit a Combined Training Event and watch the experts competing. So varied is the riding needed for the different phases of the trials that a keen young horseman will learn a great deal from watching each phase of the test and how the horses cope with the demands made upon them. It will be the ambition of every beginner to represent her own branch of the Pony Club, or Riding Club, in a team, at one of these events.

CHAPTER SIXTEEN

RIDING HOLIDAYS AND WHAT IS BEING OFFERED IN THIS SPHERE

Riding holidays have become very popular and are a healthy and enjoyable way of exploring the countryside, enjoying fresh air and exercise at the same time. There are now, however, holiday courses in bewildering variety from which to choose. Trekking, trail riding, jumping, advanced schooling and, even dressage, may be studied whilst on a riding holiday course. It is vital to investigate these possibilities first, either from personal recommendation or a visit to the proposed establishment, so that our holiday maker may gain the maximum enjoyment, both physically and mentally, from her holiday.

Before the year 1959, patrons of riding courses and pony trekking centres had no way of knowing whether the establishment they chose to visit was reputable or not. Some visitors returned from their holiday, with the uncomfortable feeling that perhaps all had not been well with the horses and ponies that they were given to ride. Being ignorant, it was difficult for them to know to whom to complain about the bad stable conditions or the ill-kept animals. So far as they were aware this might be the way that all horses were kept.

There is no doubt, alas, that some irresponsible persons did exploit the interest that riding holidays were arousing. Small, ill-equipped trekking and riding holiday stables opened up, often run by young girls totally unfit to have sole charge of half a dozen horses or to instruct would-be riders. Visitors to these establishments were given animals which, in many cases, were not up to their weight, or which showed signs of lameness, rubbed backs or girth galls and which wore ill-fitting saddles and bridles. Although the visitors did not patronise these stables again, other ignorant people did, and many riders who were enthusiastic and able were lost to the sport. 'Once bitten, twice shy' they felt and if that was all that riding holidays had to offer they would look no further.

A wonderful organisation called the Ponies of Britain Club arranged, therefore, a panel of inspectors who would visit all centres with help and advice. They awarded Certificates, as the British Horse Society now do as well, to those centres which reached the necessary standard.

It was not compulsory for a school to be inspected, but as the public became better educated to riding holidays, so they began to patronise only the establishments which could offer official recognition and the others quickly lost their patrons. It is encouraging how tremendously thorough the appointed judges are in their inspection. Horses and ponies are carefully examined for any sign of ill-health, over-work or neglect. Tack must all be clean, supple and well-fitting. Rusty curb chains, cracked leather and broken headpieces held together with string are not tolerated, incredible though it may now seem, such conditions did exist for too long before inspection became the rule.

Different types of horses and ponies are used for various holiday pursuits. Pony trekkers obviously ride ponies, these animals generally being of native hill breeds. Dressage, advanced equitation, showing and jumping courses all require horses and these animals are schooled to the work required of them.

Cross bred ponies of every variety are being used all over the country but apart from pony trekking centres, few pure bred native ponies are available for holiday riding. These ponies, which are very desirable, are also expensive, to breed and to train, and are thus chiefly found in showing and breeding studs. The exception to this is the establishment centred in the county or area where a breed or particular strain is prevalent and, therefore, reasonably abundant. For example, Fell and Highland ponies are not uncommon in riding schools and trekking centres in Northumberland, Cumberland, Westmorland and Scotland.

The Ponies of Britain Club, Brookside Farm, Ascot, have compiled a manual for the holiday rider. This is chiefly devoted to trekking,but it is helpful and to the point for anyone about to embark upon any type of riding holiday. The wonderful weekly journal, *Horse and Hound*, have produced annually a directory entitled *Holidays with Horses* which is sent free to anyone applying for it and sending a stamped addressed envelope. Although the alphabetical key directory is a bit confusing to follow it is difficult to see how else so much interesting information could have been included without making the directory a more costly affair. Anyway, any potential holiday-maker would be prepared to make time to study the manual.

Travel agencies also report record bookings for trekking and touring holidays on horseback in Europe. The demand apparently grows annually and now this department is quite a lucrative side line for some agencies. Many visitors from overseas, also, come to this island for riding holidays. This is largely thanks to the attractive qualities of our native ponies, upon whose backs the bulk of the burden quite literally rests. It now seems apparent that Britain has a wider selection of riding holiday centres than any other country. Certainly, every holiday maker who would ride should find somewhere to suit his individual needs.

Many of Britain's most attractive pony trekking and riding holiday areas lie wholly, or partially, in National Parks. It might be wise here to mention that, contrary to the view held by some riders, this does not mean that the land is 'nationalised' or completely open to the public. We cannot gallop about as though we own the land ourselves. Parts of the country which are of outstanding beauty are designated National Parks, so that they may be preserved for the nation by the exercise of certain controls on building development and the extension of existing amenities. So riders cannot wander where they will and must respect the private persons who live and work in these National Park tracts of land, always keeping to paths and tracks and never leaving litter or defacing rocks or trees with unsightly carvings. Severe penalties are now being imposed upon visitors to National Parks who leave smouldering camp fires, orange peel, and cartons, and such despicable objects behind them, and it is important that no rider should be guilty of such thoughtless conduct.

It is interesting that the Youth Hostels Association in England and Scotland now include pony trekking among the amenities offered the young people who visit them during the summer months. Trekking and accommodation is available through this organisation at only £10 a week, trekkers, in this case being responsible for their own catering.

CHAPTER SEVENTEEN

PONY TREKKING

Pony trekking is, undoubtedly, the most popular form of recreation for the holiday rider. Its chief attraction lies in the fact that it offers an admirable introduction to riding for beginners and satisfies people of all ages, tastes and degrees of riding ability. It offers a means of exploring beautiful country on sturdy, sure-footed ponies and is the type of holiday that all members of a family can enjoy.

The origin of the word 'trekking' comes from Holland and was a Cape-Dutch word commonly used by the Afrikaners to convey time or distance. When on trek, riders can go some distance and then return by nightfall to their base, probably taking a different route home. This is the commonest form of trekking. Some centres have taken this a step further and arrange overnight stops, either in hotels, farmhouses or under canvas and these are known as post-treks. Enjoyable and exciting for the riders but considerably more work for the organisers who, however, continue to do this on more ambitious lines each season because there is a demand from the public. Many delightful tours have been arranged, especially in Scotland and Wales, so that large tracts of countryside are being covered, taking in moorland and virgin terrain.

Trekking is carried out at a leisurely pace owing to the generally rough state of the ground covered and because the type of ponies used for these holidays are not built for speed. Only elementary instruction is given to the riders, who should be quite as much interested in exploring and enjoying the countryside as in riding, and in friends met and made, equine as well as human. Pony trekking is not for those who wish for more advanced instruction and some cantering and jumping.

Trekking establishments generally offer a choice of two arrangements to their guests. For those visitors who simply wish to enjoy being in the saddle for a few hours and do not wish to be troubled with any responsibility for ponies themselves, the proprietors take pride in bringing the ponies ready saddled and bridled to the hotel or stable entrance at the appointed hour for the day's trek. Some clients, however, particularly the younger ones, may enjoy the care of the ponies routine, and centres will allocate a pony to each guest at the commencement of the holiday, and expect her to be responsible for the animal's general well-being for the duration of the stay. This may entail tack-cleaning as well as grooming and feeding. A novice rider who is not fortunate enough to have her own pony will find this a particularly satisfying arrangement.

An approved trekking centre will always have a responsible rider to accompany each trek and it has already been made clear that no one who reads this book would be advised to patronise any centre which has not been so approved. Many advertisements use the term ' "expert" to accompany every ride'. This has been misleading to some pony trekking visitors and gives the mistaken impression that the leader is a real exponent in the art of horsemanship. A fallacy which needs exploding, for the rider concerned will simply be a responsible person who has riding experience and is qualified to accompany beginners and to give them help and elementary instruction, when necessary. High class teaching from an expert rider is not available at a pony trekking centre.

Rides are graded according to the guests' capabilities. There are treks of short duration for beginners and more advanced all day rides through beautiful country for those with more experience. With the revival in riding holidays during the last few years, new bridle ways and tracks are being explored and subsequently used and enjoyed in various corners of the British Isles.

It is quite astonishing the number of holiday makers who expect to go pony trekking with no adequate riding clothes at all. Elaborate garments are not necessary, in fact, a water-proof anorak is more practical than a conventional tweed jacket. A mackintosh must be purchased or borrowed, which will withstand a heavy shower but will also roll up into a neat pack to a strap in front of the saddle across the pony's withers. Strong, warm trousers will do instead of jodhpurs, corduroy are excellent. But not thin cotton jeans because they are liable to split as soon as their wearer attempts to leave the ground and gain the saddle and they are extremely cold and uncomfortable when they get wet. Children should never go on a trekking or riding holiday without a hard hat.

Saddle bags are generally used and it is not wise to carry anything on the back. A knapsack spoils every trotting stage and makes the ride more tiring. Even a little weight on the back can upset the rider's balance in an uncomfortable manner. Leave things like thermos flasks and drinking cups behind. Where there is a cottage there is a glass of water and you will be exceedingly lucky if you ride for many hours out of sight of a house.

Always carry some good quality string, a penknife and a few large spare safety pins. They may prove a blessing if a button is lost or a zip fastener breaks. A torn garment can cause severe discomfort in the saddle in wet weather. A plastic bag will be useful for putting around a camera, or protecting matches. Or even for preserving interesting flower or insect specimens if the rider is interested in collecting any wild life.

The leader of the trek will be responsible for providing first aid dressings. But the rider may like to carry her own tin of elastoplast or cold cream. Choose small tins of cream, not tubes, because the latter can get squashed and burst open. Blisters on the palms of the hands are commonplace, particularly in hot weather, and the rider may wish to be independent of the leader regarding creams and plasters.

A large white pocket handkerchief is also useful. Apart from its conventional purpose, it can, in an emergency, serve as a small bandage, or to wave as a signal if the party should get separated.

Sustaining midday lunches and hot drinks will probably be provided by the trek organiser and will be brought to the lunch rendezvous by car, or packed in convenient holders which are strapped to the saddle of a pack pony. Pony trekkers will wish to eat heartily so ignore any advice about it being wise to eat sparingly on trek. Barley sugar or good quality fruit sweets carried in the pocket are pleasant and thirst-quenching but too many toffees and sweets, other than boiled ones, will make the rider unduly thirsty.

The pony trekking season is, in the majority of centres, confined to riding from Easter until October only, the latter being a popular month, and deservedly so, as the Highlands, particularly, are known to offer the visitor beautiful cool summer days. The other winter months are too cold for the leisurely riding experienced by trekkers.

An average charge for a whole day trek at a recognised establishment is about £2 a day and £1·25 for half day.

CHAPTER EIGHTEEN

EQUIPMENT NECESSARY FOR RIDING HOLIDAYS AND PREPARATION FOR SAME. PROSPECTS FOR UNACCOMPANIED CHILDREN

Many riding establishments will now take children over eight years unescorted. These holiday courses, and what they have to offer, will appeal to many pony-loving youngsters, particularly those who are not fortunate enough to own their own ponies. There is no lack of variety offered on these courses. Proprietors are now competing with one another to offer more and varied programmes suitable for all grades of riding. Guests may choose to combine riding with a conventional holiday at a hotel as pony trekkers often do or to take things more seriously and stay at a residential riding school or a stud farm which caters for holiday visitors.

It should first be decided whether the object is to ride and enjoy the exercise and the scenery, as on trek, or whether the riding holiday is taken with the purpose of gaining experience in jumping and elementary dressage. Possibly, it would be beneficial and enjoyable to combine the two. This is feasible, but instruction will not be of a high standard if the riding school caters for a large number of guests who only wish to ride and not to be taught anything constructive.

Investigation of various riding holiday possibilities clearly indicates that it is not wise to go to a large residential school of equitation unless the visitor is anxious to do a fair amount of riding, eighteen to twenty-two hours a week is average for a school of this type. Most establishments would arrange less riding if required for individual clients but guests on these holiday courses are generally keen, dedicated types and the atmosphere is definitely 'horsey'. Perfect for the young person who loves horses and ponies and is anxious to learn more about them during her holiday and to work hard at perfecting her style in whichever branch of horsemanship she has chosen to specialise while on vacation.

Residential weekly courses at an approved top-class riding establishment run at about £40 a week. This would include the use of other facilities like the swimming pool, tennis court and other social activities arranged at the centre. Extra private lessons would be arranged if necessary at around a guinea an hour.

There are now some twenty-five first class residential schools of equitation in Great Britain where a keen student of riding could have a wonderful holiday and perfect her style of riding in whichever branch of horsemanship she chooses to specialise. Visitors come to these establishments from all over the world and the spirit and atmosphere at these centres is admirable. No one fails to learn a great deal and to obtain value for money.

There are also many good small schools of equitation, where charges for board, lodging and tuition may be less than quoted above, but the standard will not be so high, nor the subsidiary amenities available so attractive.

Young adults who are able to visit residential schools of equitation during school term times would be wise to do so. Their holiday is more likely to be quiet, constructive and generally beneficial. It is possible to arrange to take one's own horse or pony on holiday. This is a sensible arrangement, particularly if the horse is young, in need of schooling, or has just been purchased and the rider, either child or adult, is anxious to get on more intimate terms with the animal. Livery charges run, on average, at £8.40 a week for a horse and £6.30 for a pony.

Equipment necessary for a holiday of this nature is more elaborate than for pony trekking. Two pairs of jodhpurs, shirts, a tie, a mackintosh, gumboots, and a tweed jacket are necessary. If a certain amount of jumping and equitation is to be studied, breeches and boots are wise, but not essential. Anyone contemplating a holiday of this variety, anyway, will be likely to be able to ride already and should possess these garments. A hard riding hat is, of course, an essential.

A horse or pony which is attending a week or fortnight's course will require saddle, bridle, headcollar and rug, if worn. These items would travel in the horse-box with the animal. Grooming kit, stable bucket and foodstuffs are not needed where the animal is kept at livery. It need not be necessary for the owner herself to look after her pony at all where she is paying full livery fee, but she may wish to do this and arrangements can usually be made to keep the pony at a lesser charge if the visitor wishes to act as groom to her own pony.

No one should embark upon a riding course for a week without first getting into training. By this, I do not mean leisurely hacking or trekking. There is no need to get fit for this. But a rider embarking upon some intensive schooling including jumping, would be wise to prepare herself beforehand by riding regularly for a week or two. Otherwise, slack muscles may become overstrained and stiffness can be very tiring.

Children unaccompanied by parents are welcome at many establishments but in most cases they should be over twelve years of age. There are a few centres which will take them under this age but in not all the schools visited were the facilities and supervision adequate for such young children. Children on holiday naturally want to enjoy themselves. They will ride as much as possible if they are keen enough to go on a holiday of this nature. They will explore the amenities of the neighbourhood and retire to bed as late as adult supervision will allow. They must, therefore, go somewhere which has been visited beforehand and has been personally recommended. Reasonable supervision of riding, meal times, bed times and companions, is essential for all youngsters staying alone away from home.

It is important to find a centre which takes trouble to employ the children out of riding hours and which provides suitable supplementary recreations. The more expensive residential schools can offer swimming, tennis, table tennis and dancing on the premises and will take young people on occasional trips to places of interest in the neighbourhood. Small centres, and non-residential ones attached to hotels, are often not so well equipped, so it is important to make preliminary enquiries about what there is for young people to do and, also, how much and how capable, the supervision which is provided for the young.

Riding holidays in Britain, as distinct from trekking, do prove to be, on investigation, many and varied in what they offer the young rider. Practically every proprietor, to whom enquiries were made, was co-operative and helpful and anxious to please the potential holiday maker. But the few exceptions where the riding tuition and care of the horses was not of a high standard and young visitors were working unnecessarily long hours as 'holiday' grooms, do serve to illustrate how important it is to be recommended to an establishment by a friend who either lives near and knows the place from visits, or better still, who has been on holiday there.

In an early March issue of *Horse and Hound*, this excellent publication generally devotes several pages to advertisements of trekking and riding holiday centres, and there is a wealth of interesting holiday courses offered in different parts of the country.

Horse drawn caravans can now be seen on the country roads during holiday periods. These relics of the past are not so easily found today and when they are discovered, generally tucked away in farmyards, they are likely to be being used to house chickens or farm tools and are not road worthy. Nevertheless, these vans are being renovated by a few enthusiasts and, provided the hull remains intact, new wheels and shafts can be fitted. Generally horse drawn van roofs are made of wood and canvas, both of which can be repaired, or renewed, if necessary, by any carpenter. The inside of the vans are surprisingly spacious, whole families having lived in them in the past while they travelled from one end of the country to the other. The pace is slow but the unhurried mode of life very pleasant, there is warmth and a degree of comfort when the elements are unkind and it is delightful for children to wander from the van to examine or watch anything of interest that is passed, and then to catch up with the vehicle when they wish.

Twelve to fifteen miles makes a comfortable day's journey with a horse caravan. As with all trekking holidays, arrangements have to be made about overnight accommodation in advance. Not every farmer or landowner is willing to allow an unknown horse amongst his T.T. tested herds or in fields to be grazed by them. Also, of course, a route avoiding all busy roads will have to be worked out, although, alas, these are becoming more and more difficult to find these days.

CHAPTER NINETEEN

ODDS AND ENDS TO DO WITH THE HORSE WORLD

An interesting venture that has been promoted by riding enthusiasts in Great Britain is the Golden Horse Shoe Ride, a cross-country exercise over an average of sixty miles of all types of country. For this event, qualifying rides are now being held all over the country and are arousing great interest, and many enthusiastic competitors. Here is a field in which our novice rider, and her pony, with whom she should now be on good terms, will be able to take part with confidence. Because these rides are not races, but endurance rides over rough going, as well as smooth, and participants take part for their own pleasure and satisfaction and not for financial or material gain.

Thus it will be seen that the field of activities for our rider and her mount is now wide open and scope is endless. During most months of the year there will be some event organised nearby in which she can take part, and there is always hunting, which is the greatest fun of all.

Horse and Hound is a weekly newspaper for the horseman, and for the price of 12½p it will keep the rider up to date with all that is going on, in every branch of horsemanship, in the country. There is, in it, details of most equine fixtures of note in every area. Even the advertisements make interesting reading for the novice rider.

When a pony is bought, it is a sensible plan to insure him against accident. No one needs reminding of the high cost of a good mount and if a fatality does occur, then some hard-won savings will disappear as well. A vet's fees can mount alarmingly in the case of sickness and this will not be covered, but, in the case of death, if the animal is insured, it will not be quite such a strain on the family finances if it becomes necessary to go out and buy another one. Perhaps this sounds a very unlikely possibility, and one which is certainly not going to confront our hopeful beginner, but, alas, horses and ponies are flesh and blood, and anyone who has owned a pony or ponies will tell you that they can, and do, sometimes come to an untimely end.

It is important to insure for the correct amount. It is necessary to give the name, age, sex and value of the pony to the insurers. They may also ask for a veterinary certificate, to the effect that the pony is sound in wind and limb, and some details of the general use to which it will be put. Premium costs average something like £7 to £10 per annum for a pony valued at £100. Some insurers may agree on a lower fee per annum if the pony is not going to be used for hunting or jumping, but we sincerely hope that our novice's pony is going to indulge in these two delightful pastimes.

Hazards there are today in plenty and the highways provide their fair share. So does the increasing use of modern agricultural fertilising methods which do not always agree with a pony's digestive system and which cause all sorts of tiresome, and sometimes fatal, diseases, like laminitis and grass ill and even heart strain. Ponies, in their natural habitat, did not need richly treated pasture to survive, and to thrive, and it does not always suit them.

The world of horses has come to have a language of its own among those connected with it, and, although familiar to those who work amongst horses, it may not be so clear to the recruit.

The language of some of the old and crusted dealers, of which it is heartening to report there are still a few characters in business, holds expressions many of which are individual to themselves, and would even puzzle learned folk who have spent a lifetime with ponies.

One delightful, but very obscure expression, used by dealers who do not wish to buy a certain animal, is that he is 'too much given to writing home'. No one could possibly guess that the dealer had observed this animal in the stable

131

Fig. 25. This horse has all the faults – lop ears, Roman nose, ewe neck, calf-kneed and goose-rumped

pointing a fore foot forward in a way suggesting one of the deadliest ailments of all, navicular disease. Another expression which will condemn a horse, is to hear him described by an old hand as a 'fly-catcher'. This term describes a good-looking, but worthless animal, such as no dealer would wish to have through his hands. A more flattering description is 'there's a fox-catcher' – and this, of course, conveys the opposite meaning to the above and denotes a horse worth buying which should make a good hunter.

There are more expressions of this nature, the explanation of which is beyond the scope of this book, but the above will serve to illustrate just how odd some of them are.

The veterinary surgeon will describe unsoundnesses such as splints, spavins, thoroughpin, ring bones and side bones. But it is useful to be able to recognise a horse which 'makes a noise'. This may be only a minor defect and is caused by the atrophy of one, or sometimes, both, of the muscles whose business it is to open and close the larynx in the action of breathing, the sound resulting from the air passing the obstruction caused by this. Quite a few people put up with this in an otherwise good horse but do not have anything to do with a 'broken-winded' animal. Broken-wind is a serious affection of the lungs preventing them performing their function as the pump inhaling and exhaling the breath.

'Curby hocks' refers to a particular shape of hock which is liable to develop curbs, a bony formation causing unsoundness. 'Cow hocked' refers to hind legs again and its meaning is surprisingly difficult to trace, and is not flattering to the cow, but upon investigation it seems to relate to hocks which are nearer together than they should be.

'Calf-kneed' again refers back to the unfortunate cow but is a more serious description and in my humble opinion a horse described thus is one to be avoided at all costs. Literally described, 'calf-kneed' means 'back at the knee' so that an imaginary line taken side view down the centre of the fore arm to the ground, instead of passing through the middle of the fetlock joint as it should, would emerge below the knee and reached the ground behind the heel. Obviously, this shape will subject the back tendons to undue strain and consequent liability to injury.

The opposite fault 'over at the knee' although unsightly is far less objectionable, and many horses and ponies have been that shape since birth and not too much the worse for it in action.

Legs are, of course, the common seat of trouble. 'No foot, no horse' is all too true. The above, are only a few of the less obscure that should be mentioned, and even these come dangerously near to the province of the veterinary surgeon. It is interesting, however, to know the meaning of these phrases when attending horse sales which are fascinating affairs from which much about horses and their conformation may be learnt.

'Loaded shoulders' is an expression denoting thick and generally rather upright shoulders, a shape which seldom goes with the freedom so necessary to galloping and jump-

Fig. 26. Dishfaced. Roman nosed

ing. 'Goose-rumped' is curious, because research does not prove the term to have relation to any characteristic noticeable in the goose. It does, in fact, describe a horse whose tail is set on low. The reverse may be seen in the Arab which has its tail almost abnormally high.

'Dishfaced' is not an attractive term but does, in fact, describe the lovely line of the Arab face which shows a slight break about halfway between the eyes and nose. This is very marked even in some thoroughbreds who must have inherited this type of head from their original Eastern Ancestors. The reverse term a 'roman nose' is much less attractive and almost invariably denotes a throw back to a hairy heeled strain in the pedigree. Heavy horses used in agriculture nearly always carried this striking characteristic, and very handsome they looked, but it is not becoming in the lighter breeds.

'Lop ears' need little explanation but are undoubtedly a curiosity because there have been some remarkably good blood lines in which this characteristic keeps recurring. It gives the horse a foolish dull look but this is often proved not to be a true indication of the animal's character. Lop ears, therefore, need not put off any prospective buyer of an otherwise good animal.

'Ewe-necked' refers, of course, to a fancied resemblance

to a sheep. Farmyard animals and their characteristics have obviously been freely adopted, and abused, by the equine world. This term may also be described as 'having his neck put on upside down' the upper lines being concave instead of convex. It may, in fact, be an unsightly malformation and a difficult one to erase from a blood line. Whereas an arched neck is more a result of carriage got through breaking and handling, except in the case of stallions of some age which grow a crest indicative of mature masculine character.

There are, necessarily, many terms omitted from these notes, but these are a few which may prove useful to the beginner.

A little Veterinary knowledge may prove to be a dangerous thing and there are plenty of books which deal with first-aid for the horse owner. Except in very simple cases it is better to call in skilled advice and when the veterinary surgeon does come, do pick his brains and glean as much information as you can. A visit from the vet is quite an expensive luxury and not to be wasted in idle conversation. Most vets, anyway, are friendly and helpful to novice owners.

A vigilant eye and a thorough understanding of your pony's general behaviour, his habits and stable manners, will help the inexperienced owner-groom to detect the first signs of uneasiness or distress. By this means she can seek professional advice before the trouble really takes hold and becomes serious.

Riding really is a valuable means of character training. It is noticeable how some young people are inclined to treat a horse like a motor car and desire at first only to get speed and work out of it. Then week by week one notices them developing a feeling for the horse as a sentient creature, until finally they display a new sympathy and understanding which, we hope, will extend itself to other aspects of life. When that time comes, not only will they get a better ride, but they will be better people and easier to live with.

Increased joy in the countryside and a greater love for

Fig. 27. A vigilant eye will help the owner-groom to detect the first signs of uneasiness and distress

nature at every season of the year can surely be regarded as a species of character training and where can one develop these better than from the back of a pony? Riding tempts us out in all weathers so that we learn to enjoy the wind and rain as well as the sun and warm breezes.

Concentration and quick thinking are of importance both on the pony's back and in the stable. Listen to the difference between a groom's footstep and a gardener's. The former, if it belongs to a real horseman or woman, will be quick, light and alert. This power of concentration, acquired and fostered by riding, may easily extend itself to other activities, to the subsequent benefit of the young person.

INDEX

Beginner's Guide to Coarse Fishing

ARTHUR E. HARDY

Whether you take up coarse fishing for sport, relaxation or pure pleasure, a good 'starter' book can go a long way to eliminating some of the guesswork, explain the mysteries of modern fishing tackle and spell out, in simple detail, the wide variety of baits, methods and other 'wrinkles' that could mean the difference between a blank day and a worthwhile catch.

This is such a book. The easy to follow text takes the novice step by step into the watery world of each species of coarse fish – how, when and where it feeds and the right tackle, baits and methods for its successful and most sporting capture.

Sphere   40p

Beginner's Guide to Tropical Fish and Fish Tanks

REGINALD DUTTA

Techniques improve very rapidly in this thriving, fast
changing industry – aerators, filters, tanks, heating and
lighting are clear examples, and you need to be guided by
a man who really knows the field. This book is produced
from within the very heart of the industry; the author is the
Managing Director of London's oldest-established tropical
fish specialists. The book is written from the customer's
point of view. Its information and guidance will save many
a needless headache and useless expense, and make your
tank pleasant and pleasing.

Sphere   40p

Beginner's Guide to Painting in Oils

BARBARA DORF

This original and helpful book is designed to help anyone starting oil painting to create pictures that are entirely their own. Rules that are given are only guides, and can be broken if the result is a good, individual painting.

Extensive information is given on the many aspects of oil painting materials and techniques. The many line illustrations and diagrams in the text make points clearer and easier to follow.

There is something here for everyone who wishes to paint, and oil painting is approached as something to give satisfaction and pleasure to both painter and onlooker.

Sphere   40p